Tilda's
FAIRY TALE
WONDERLAND

Tone Finnanger

David and Charles

www.stitchcraftcreate.co.uk

Preface

In a world where time is passing by very quickly, it is easy to get nostalgic. Your thoughts go back to childhood where, with a little imagination, the world seemed magical and everything was possible. Your daily routine seemed unchangeable and everlasting and you were at the centre of the universe, living in the certain knowledge that everything would remain the same forever. With this book, I wanted to go back and find that childish sense of security, joy and excitement.

Some of the memories I have brought into light and worked on are my grandmother's Danish-inspired Christmas, a Christmas decorated amusement park in Copenhagen and stories and fairy tales that created magic in everyday life. I also recalled memories of grown-up's parties where everything was sparkling and you almost became invisible between suit-legs and beautiful hemlines. It's all about bringing back happy memories and those magical moments where you were carefree and happy.

My childhood was full of stories that made an indelible impression. To find figures for the book, I brought back many of the old stories that characterized my childhood, and hopefully the childhood of many others too. Good stories and fairy tales can reach children all over the world and run in generations. They become history, but also touch the lives of children today.

While working on this book I read a number of the old fairy tales and stories again with an adult's point of view, and even though some of the fairy tales are surprisingly horrific, it has been a pleasant task. You can never fit everything you want into a book, but I selected suitable figures and scenes to use as décor throughout.

It is lovely to relive stories from your childhood and to sew fairy tale figures as toys. Many of the fairy tale-inspired figures also naturally lend themselves to a Christmas décor theme. I hope that you enjoy making the projects as much as I have creating them.

Tone Finnanger

Contents

Materials

Tilda fabrics and materials have been used to make the models in this book. The fabrics are mainly from the Tilda Quilt Collection, however there are many additional Tilda fabrics in the range.

Fabrics in The Tilda Quilt Collection have a width of 110cm (44in) and are of a thinner quality than some of the previous Tilda fabrics, making them easier to use for small models and miniatures. On larger models, this is less important and any Tilda fabrics can be used. Use one-coloured Tilda fabrics as skin for the different figures.

Cotton wadding (batting) is used on hand-quilted models and Panduro's synthetic stuffing wadding is recommended for use in the stuffed figures.

You can find the cardboard, wrapping paper, paper décor, silk paper, ribbons and buttons that are used in the book among the Tilda products. The same goes for doll's hair, face-making sets, figure stands and similar accessories. The equipment used to make the Christmas marzipan can be purchased at a variety of well-assorted kitchen supply stores.

www.tildasworld.com

www.ilovetilda.com

Stuffed figures

Making solid templates out of cardboard is recommended. Paper templates do not keep their shape and can leave you with an inaccurate result.

Do not cut out the parts before you sew, but iron the fabric twice, trace the pattern and sew around it. Then cut the parts with a 3–4mm (⅛–¼in) seam allowance by the seams and a 10–12mm (⅜–½in) seam allowance by the openings. It is important to cut notches in the seam allowance where it curves inwards. Make sure that you loosen seam allowances that are sewn to the seams on parts where two or more fabrics are sewn together.

Turn the parts inside out using a flower stick or similar. It is a good idea to keep wooden sticks in different sizes for this purpose.

To reverse slim legs and arms, push the blunt end of a stick against the tip of the arm/leg, see figure A. Start closest to the foot/hand and pull the leg/

arm down the wooden stick, see figure B. Grab the foot/hand and pull whilst holding the bottom to turn the leg/arm inside out, see figure C.

Iron the reversed parts thoroughly and iron the seam allowance inwards, as described in the instructions.

Stuff the parts using your fingers where possible and wooden sticks where you can't reach. The figures should now be stuffed well.

It is important to insert the wadding (batting) loosely into the figure to avoid lumps. If you find that two lumps of wadding will not lie next to each other and an air pocket is created, stick a large needle through the fabric and twist until the wadding has loosened up and the lumps are merged into each other.

You will find further instructions in the different projects in the book.

A   B   C

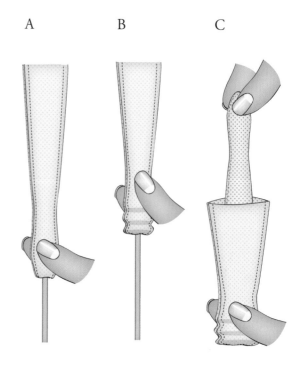

Miniatures

Small figures, such as the Little Ballerina on page 34, the Teaspoon Ladies on page 48, the Miniature Animals on page 94 and the Little Princess on page 117, can seem a little challenging to make. However, they are very cute in their miniature size and you are certain to cherish them once they are created.

If you find making miniatures is not for you, it is easy to enlarge the patterns and create the figures at a larger size.

It is the reversing of the miniature figures that is particularly challenging. You cannot use your fingers to the same extent; instead you will need to work with a small wooden pin. It is useful to try to find an even thinner stick than a flower stick to work with, for example a baking stick or similar. The rest is fairly easy, just working on a smaller scale.

When you reverse the small arms and legs, the challenge is to divide the layers of fabric from each other to be able to go through with the reversing technique shown with figures A, B and C on page 10. Do this by sticking a wooden pin in the arm/leg to make a hollow between the layers of fabric, see figure D. Then remove the pin and push it against the tip of the arm/leg, see figure E.

You have to work carefully to get the little tip to reverse inwards. If you don't succeed the first time, try again. The most challenging part is over when the pieces are reversed. Press the pieces using the tip of the iron and stuff with the help of a small wooden pin.

D   E

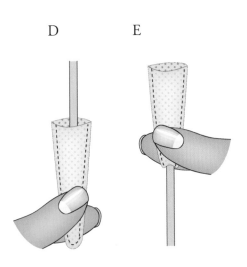

Hair

When working on a figure, always begin with the hair, so you can adjust the face thereafter without touching it too much.

PAINTED HAIR

Many of the figures in this book have painted black hair, inspired by old porcelain dolls. To create this you will need a vanishing fabric pen, matt black craft paint and a small flat brush; size 2–4 is a good size. Paint from the Tilda face kit (ref. no. 713400) is also used here.

Begin drawing the outline of the hair with a vanishing fabric pen, following the pattern. Then paint the outline, using plenty of paint on the brush and adding the curves one by one.

The fabric will soak in some paint, so dip the brush often. Try to make the edges as even as possible and then fill inside the outline, see figure A.

Lean the figure towards a glass or similar until the hair is completely dry.

OTHER HAIR

The Teaspoon Ladies are the only figures in this book that have the regular Tilda hair. Since these figures are so small, you only need to push one large pin right through the head, or use a small pin on each side of the head to attach the hair.

Attach the end of the yarn on one of the sides and position the yarn in a curve over the head where you want the hairline by the forehead to be. Continue from one pin to the other through the neck.

Attach the yarn with a few tacking (basting) stitches and pull out the pin. Continue looping in a circular motion until the head is covered, see figure B. Use as little hair as possible so that the hair doesn't end up too big for the small head.

Make two small hairballs, measuring approximately 1.5cm (⅝in) in diameter, and tack the balls fairly high up on each side of the head, see figure C.

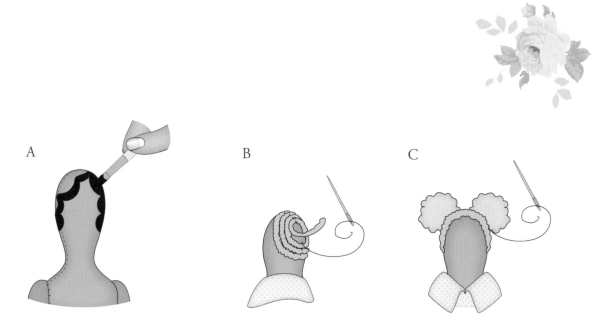

A

B

C

Faces

Push two pins into the head to see where you want to position the eyes. Remove the pins. Using the eye tool from the Tilda face kit (ref. no. 713400) or the head of a small pin, dip into black paint and stamp the eyes where you have marked the holes.

Apply Tilda blusher, lipstick or similar with a dry brush to make the cheeks look rosy.

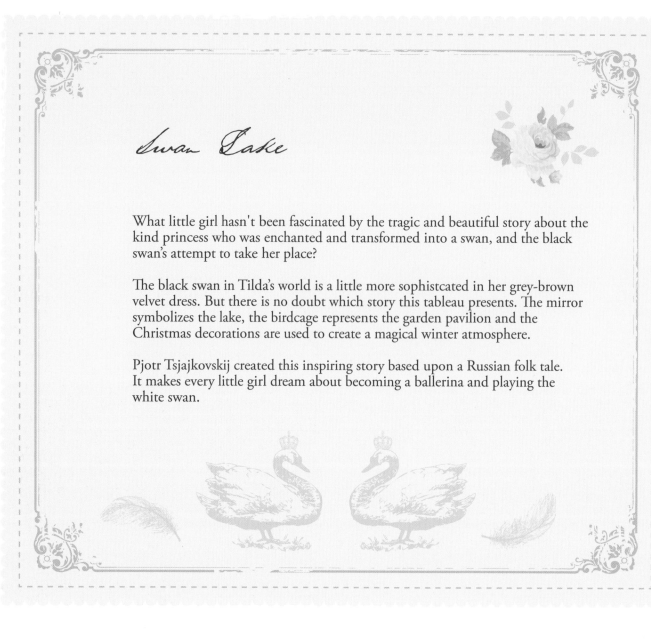

Swan Lake

What little girl hasn't been fascinated by the tragic and beautiful story about the kind princess who was enchanted and transformed into a swan, and the black swan's attempt to take her place?

The black swan in Tilda's world is a little more sophistcated in her grey-brown velvet dress. But there is no doubt which story this tableau presents. The mirror symbolizes the lake, the birdcage represents the garden pavilion and the Christmas decorations are used to create a magical winter atmosphere.

Pjotr Tsjajkovskij created this inspiring story based upon a Russian folk tale. It makes every little girl dream about becoming a ballerina and playing the white swan.

Ballerinas

HOW TO MAKE

Read the instructions about how to make stuffed figures on page 10.

If you use a delicate velvet fabric for the ballet dress and shoes, such as silk velvet or similar, it can be a good idea to iron thin iron-on woven interfacing (Vlieseline) on the wrong side of the fabric before you start.

Body
Fold the skin fabric in half and trace the body and two arms. Sew together a wide strip of skin fabric and a slim strip of the fabric for the shoes, so that the border between the fabrics will be approximately where it is marked in the pattern. The sewn-together strip needs to accommodate two legs when it is folded right sides together. Trace the legs from the pattern.

YOU WILL NEED

Tilda skin fabric
Fabric for the dress and shoes
Equipment for the hair, see page 12
Pearls and buttons
Wadding (batting)

See pattern on pages 138–139.

Sew around all the pieces. Leave the opposite corners at the bottom of the body open, but attach each end together at the bottom with a few stitches, see figure A.

Cut out all the pieces and fold the corners on the upper body opposite, so that you can sew right across on each side, see figure B. Reverse, fold in the seam allowance by the openings and iron all of the pieces.

Stuff all the parts. Put the legs inside the body, attach with pins and tack (baste) in place, see figure C.

Cut a strip of dress fabric measuring approximately 16 × 5cm (6⅜ × 2in) with the seam allowance included. Fold the top edges inwards and tack the fabric strip tightly around the chest to create the waist of the dress. Make a few cuts at the bottom of the strip if you wish to make the dress tighter around the waist, see figure D.

A

B

C

D

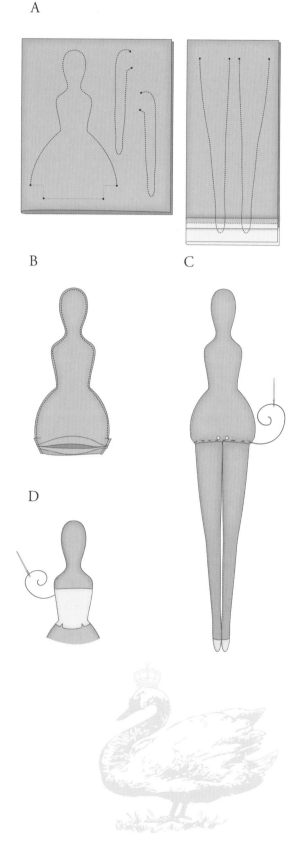

Attach the arms close to the body with pins, so that the openings are around the shoulders and attach with tacking stitches, see figure E.

I recommend that you paint the hair, as described on page 12, before you dress the doll. This way there is less of chance of staining on the dress.

Skirt

The strip to the skirt should be 15cm (6in) wide, cut without seam allowance so that the running edge is visible. The length will depend on the type of fabric that you choose. If you use a thin cotton fabric as I have here for the light dress, the length of the strip could be the whole fabric width, 110–140cm (44–55in). If you use velvet, 100cm (40in) should be enough.

Crumple the fabric around the ballerina and attach with pins. The skirt should have a lot of volume, but it should not consist of more fabric than you are able to pucker up around the waist.

Stitch up the two short ends and turn the skirt inside out. Tack along the edge on top of the skirt, tighten the tacked edge around the waist of the ballerina and attach, see figure F.

You can also sew a row of small mother of pearl buttons or pearls along the top edge if you wish.

Shoes

Use strips of the same fabric that is used for the dress to make the tie ribbons for the ballet shoes. Cutting strips with the help of cutting equipment for quilting is recommended, but you can also cut strips with scissors or use a narrow ribbon. You will need a strip that is 6–7mm (¼in) wide and 65cm (26in) long for each shoe.

Fold the middle of the strip and attach on the back of the shoe, see figure G. Wind the two strip ends around and upwards from the foot so that they cross each other three times on the front side, see photo (right).

Tie a bow on the outside of the leg and attach with a few stitches to prevent it from slipping down.

Hair band

Cut a 1.5 × 7cm (⅝ × 2¾in) strip with seam allowances included. Fold the edges inwards to make the strip 7mm (¼in) wide, and attach tightly over the head with a pin on each side.

Tack along the edge of the strip on each side to keep the seam allowance in place, attaching the strip, see figure H.

Cut two 2.5 × 10cm (1 × 4in) strips and sew little flower embellishments as described on page 120. Tack a flower to each side of the head, so the ends of the strip that is attached over the head will be hidden, see figure I. Make the face as described on page 13.

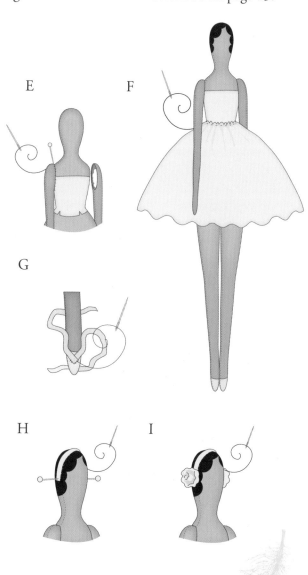

E   F

G

H   I

It is difficult to make a book without any roses; they are beautiful embellishments and are so easy to make.

Vintage roses

HOW TO MAKE

Cut a strip measuring 10cm (4in) × the whole fabric width. Soak in water for a couple of minutes then knead it with your hands to make a little ball. Wind the strip carefully out so that it maintains as many wrinkles as possible. Hang to dry.

When the strip is dry, fold it in half with the right side outwards. Also fold down one of the corners, see figure A.

Wind the strip loosely around and around until you have a loose rose shape. Be careful to keep the wrinkles and shape the rose on a flat table surface.

While the rose still is on the table, thread the doll needle with embroidery yarn right through all the layers. Sew 4–5 times in different directions through the whole rose without tightening too much. The end result is a beautifully textured rose that can be used to decorate many projects.

YOU WILL NEED

Fabric for the rose
Doll needle
Embroidery yarn

A

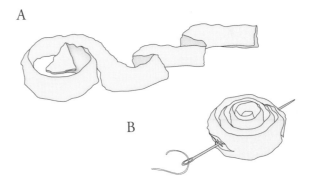

B

Ballerina Christmas stocking

HOW TO MAKE

The focus is on the front of the stocking. Use the same fabric on the back as for the stocking itself, without the appliquéd shoe and ribbon. Wadding (batting) is used only on the front side.

If you wish to appliqué on both sides, make another piece in the same way as the front piece, this time in reverse.

The pattern is divided into three pieces to fit the pattern pages. Place the pattern together so that points A and B are next to each other and repeat with points C and D.

It is important to add a seam allowance to the front piece, as it should be appliquéd and quilted. Cut two opposite/reversed stocking pieces in the stocking fabric and two pieces in the lining fabric. Also cut a piece of the stocking in wadding for the front.

YOU WILL NEED

Fabric for the stocking and loop
Fabric for the lining
Fabric for the shoe and
tie ribbon
Cotton wadding (batting)
Stuffing wadding

See pattern on pages 140–141.

If you find it difficult to quilt, the stocking looks great without it too.

Appliqué

Trace and cut out the shoe from the pattern, adding a seam allowance measuring about 1cm (⅜in) around the edge. Cut a notch along the edge where the shoe will meet the stocking. Fold and iron the edge inwards, see figure A.

Use a scissors or a cutter to cut out a strip measuring 2.5cm × 1m (1 × 40in). Iron approximately 7mm (¼in) inwards on each side so the strip will measure 1cm (⅜in) wide.

Place the strip so that the bottom part of the ribbon is marked in the pattern and cut a suitable length. Make sure that you add approximately 1cm (⅜in) on each side of the strip. Continue until you have all the parts for the appliquéd tie ribbon.

Place the parts for the tie ribbon and shoe against the stocking fabric piece. Attach with pins. Make sure that the side of the tie ribbon that is lying against the shoe is positioned beneath its edge.

Use a sewing machine to stitch a 6mm (¼in) seam in the middle of the tie ribbon and along the folded in edge on the shoe. The only purpose of the seams is to keep the pieces in place while you sew by hand, so do not attach the thread.

Remove the pins and place the appliquéd part against the wadding part. Iron before you attach the fabric and wadding together with pins, see figure B.

Tack (baste) small stitches along both sides of the tie ribbons and along the edge of the shoe. Pull out the large seam.

The stocking on page 27 is quilted, simply through wadding and fabric. Just by pulling the thread lightly while quilting, you will achieve a great result. The alternative is to quilt after the stocking is made or to use an extra layer of lining. Quilt 2–3mm (⅛in) outside the edge on each side of the tie ribbons and outside the shoe edge, see figure C.

Stitch the lining parts to the top back of the fabric and appliquéd parts, see figure D. Place the two sewn-together parts right sides together and sew around. Leave a reverse opening in the lining part, see figure E.

Cut any extra seam allowance and make notches in the seam allowance where the seam curves inwards. Turn the stocking inside out, push the linin down in the stocking part and iron. Push some wadding all the way down to the bottom to shape the shoe.

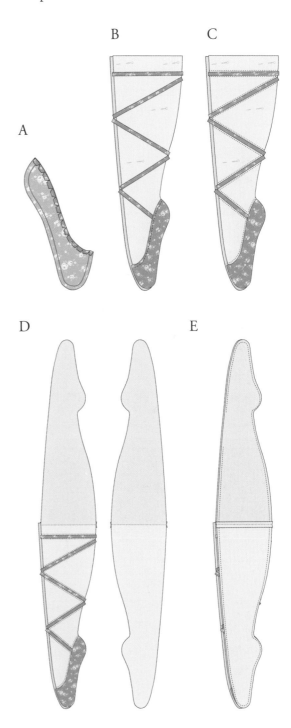

Loop and bow

Cut a strip measuring 3.5cm × 1m (1⅜ × 40in) for the bow and a strip measuring 3.5 × 25cm (1⅜ × 10in) for the loop. Fold and iron each short end approximately 1cm (⅜in) inwards.

Fold and iron approximately 7mm (¼in) inwards along each long side then fold and iron the strips in half so that they will become approximately 1cm (⅜in) wide. Stitch up the open side by hand or machine. Fold the loop and tack the ends to the inside of the stocking.

Make a bow from the long strip and attach with tacking stitches, see photo (right). Stuff some wadding all the way down to the bottom of the shoe before filling it up with gifts and sweets.

A brooch or similar can be attached to decorate the tip of the shoe.

Mini bulletin board

YOU WILL NEED

Materials for the board (see below), cotton wadding (batting), fabric, string, buttons and embroidery yarn (optional), staple gun.

HOW TO MAKE

Here I have used an insulating board that can easily be cut with a utility knife and can be found at most timber stockists. You can also use a canvas frame in your desired size. The star bulletin board (left) measures 14 × 19cm (5½ × 7½in) and the floral board (right) measures 19 × 27cm (7½ × 10¾in).

Use a stapler and attach the insert wadding first then wrap the fabric tightly around the board/ frame. Attach string around the board (see left) or sew buttons onto the frame and attach string between the buttons (see right). If you wish, you can cover the back with fabric, tacking to the fabric and wadding along the outer edge.

A bulletin board is usually associated with something useful,
but these small boards also make great decorations.

The steadfast tin soldier

Hans Christian Andersen's sad story of love between the fragile ballerina and the insignificant, one-legged tin soldier has made a lasting impression on many. The tin soldier is lost, but due to his steadfastness and bravery, he is finally reunited with his love. Despite her braveness and his steadfastness, the story ends in heatbreak. Maybe they are together forever after all.

A specific scene of this story stuck in my mind: the description of a toy that was displayed on a table. It is partly recreated here with a small paper house, which symbolizes the ballerina's castle, and a porcelain swan that can remind us of the little lake full of swans. The figures are easy to recognize; the little ballerina with her blue ribbon and the steadfast, one-legged tin soldier with his amorous glance.

Little ballerina

HOW TO MAKE

The pattern for the Little Ballerina is similar to the pattern for the Little Princess on page 117, however the details needed for the arms and legs to stand as they do requires a little more work. If you think this is too complicated, you can sew the body of the Little Ballerina with arms and legs down, by using the Little Princess pattern. Read more about miniatures on page 11.

Body

Sew the legs in the same way as for the Ballerinas on page 19.

Fold the fabric for the body and arms in half and trace the parts from the pattern. Note the curve on one of the sides of the body and that the reverse opening only holds one leg.

Turn all the pieces inside out and fold the seam allowance inwards at the bottom of the body, by the openings on the arms and on one of the legs. Iron all the pieces.

See pattern on page 142.

Stuff the body and legs. Leave the seam allowance on the non-folded leg, inwards in the opening on the body and tack (baste), see figure A. Add hair to the figure, following the instructions on page 12.

The waist of the dress is made the same way as for the Ballerinas on page 19, using a strip measuring approximately 5 × 11cm (2 × 4⅜in). Attach the other leg to the body with tacking stitches, see figure B.

Arms

To make the arms hold their position, bend a piece of wire measuring about 25cm (10in) in half and twist. Make a loop at one of the ends, see figure C. Thread the wire into the arm and use a flower stick or similar to help stuff around, see figure D. Shape the arm as in figure E.

Push the wire together and twist into the shoulder of the figure. Tack around the opening to attach the arm around the shoulder, see figure F.

Skirt

Sew the skirt in the same way as for the Ballerinas on page 19, using a strip measuring 10 × 75cm (4 × 30in) .

Hair decorations

Make hair decorations in the same way as for the Ballerinas on page 19, using a strip measuring 1 × 5cm (⅜ × 2in) over the head, so that it will only have a width of 5mm (¼in) when the edges are folded in. The rosette flowers are made here with strips measuring approximately 1.5 × 7cm (⅝ × 2¾in).

Shoes

Cut a piece of embroidery yarn measuring approximately 35cm (14in) for each leg. Sew the yarn through the shoe and leave the same length outside the shoe. Twist the yarn up the leg and let it cross over twice. Make a bow on the outer side of the leg and attach with a few stitches to make sure the yarn doesn't slip.

Ribbon

The ribbon is made in the same way as the loop for the Ballerina Christmas stocking on page 26, this time using a strip measuring 25 × 2.5cm (10 × 1in). Fold approximately 5mm (¼in)

inwards on each side and fold in half so the strip becomes approximately 7mm (¼in) wide. Attach diagonally across the body, see figure G.

Make a face, as described on page 13.

Little ballerina makes a cute hanging decoration or looks great on top of the Christmas tree...

This tin soldier is both steadfast and romantic with the little rose on his chest. A true hero.

One-legged tin soldier

HOW TO MAKE

Body

Cut strips measuring 18cm (7in) in height with a width equal to that of the hat, face and shoe in the pattern, adding a seam allowance. Cut a piece measuring 13.5cm (5¼in) and a piece measuring 4.5cm (1¾in) in width for the jacket. The height should be equal to the area marked for jacket in the pattern. Add a seam allowance.

A

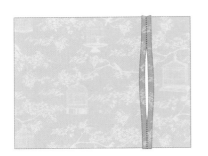

Stitch up the two parts, but leave a 5cm (2in) opening in the seam for reversing and stuffing, see figure A.

See pattern on page 144.

Sew all the strips together. It is important to be precise, so that the borders between the different pieces are approximately where they are marked in the pattern.

Iron the seam allowance away from each other and iron the strip in half, right sides together. Trace the body from the pattern and sew around, see figure B.

Arms

Stitch up the fabric for the hands in the same way. Fold right sides together, trace the arms and sew around, see figure C.

Cut out the body and arms. It is important to cut loose the seam allowances that are sewn to avoid tension, see figure D.

Reverse, iron and stuff all the parts. Stitch up the reverse opening.

If you want the arms to move back and forth, it is a good idea to use a doll needle. Sew from one arm to the other through the body, see figure E. Tighten the embroidery yarn and attach.

Embellishments

Paint the hair, as described on page 12.

Cut two strips measuring 16 × 1.5cm (6¼ × ⅝in) for the ribbons over the shoulders and a strip measuring 12 × 2cm (4½ × ¾in) for the belt. Fold the edges inwards so the shoulder ribbons become 7–8mm (⅜in) wide and the belt 9–10mm (½in) wide. Attach the ribbons and belt with pins and tack. Finished ribbons can be used instead of fabric as an easier alternative.

Here I have sewn stitches with red embroidery yarn to decorate the ribbons and belt.

Cut a strip measuring 8 × 1.5cm (3¼ × ⅝in), fold the edges inwards to make a width of 7–8mm (⅜in) and attach the strip around the neck as a collar.

The two curves marked in the pattern are embroidered with red embroidery yarn to decorate the hat, see figure F. Attach a small rose with some adhesive if you wish.

Make the face, as described on page 13. You can find figure stands in the Tilda collection.

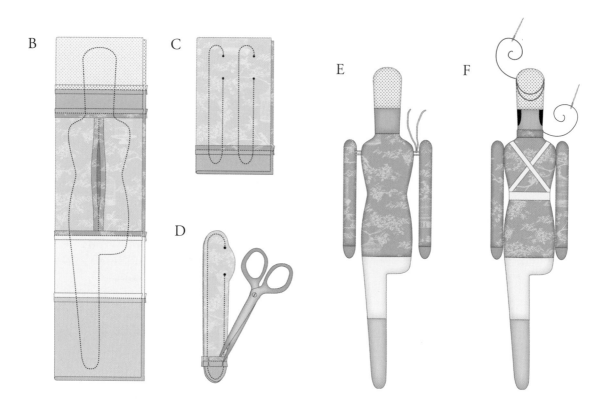

B   C

D

E   F

A velvet heart is sewn from the pattern onto the Nightshirt hearts on page 123 and decorated with paper embellishments.

Wrapping paper and fabric can be found in the Tilda collection.

Beautiful Christmas marzipan is made with the help of kitchen mould equipment (see page 8) and then brushed with edible glitter.

The Teaspoon Lady

It's not easy to do everything that should be done when you shrink to the size of a teaspoon as soon as your husband leaves the house. The teaspoon lady makes the impossible possible by using her connections to get it all done. Many people would be familiar with having to face challenges in a short amount of time and how it somehow seems to work out just in time.

This Tilda-version appears a little nervous with her pretty dress and flower in her hair. The expression on her small face reveals her shock at transforming into the size of a teaspoon.

The popular stories of *The Teaspoon Lady* are written by Alf Prøysen and have been translated to twenty-three languages.

The perfect size to rest in a pretty little teacup.

Teaspoon ladies

Old porcelain teacups are widely accessible for a cheap price from flea markets. Tiny, fragile ones are best suited for the little Teapot Ladies. Read more about miniatures on page 11.

HOW TO MAKE

Body
Fold the fabric for the body and arms right sides together and trace the parts from pattern. Sew around, cut out, reverse, iron and fill. Iron the seam allowance by the arm openings inwards and fill the arms.

See pattern on pages 140–141.

See pattern on pages 140–141.

YOU WILL NEED

Tilda skin fabric
Fabric for the dress
Tilda hair or similar
Small porcelain teacup
Roses and wings to decorate (optional)
Wadding (batting)
Glue gun

Sew a seam with tacking (basting) stitches around the cup opening with embroidery yarn or double thread. It is not necessary to fold in the seam allowance, since the bottom will not be visible. Fill the body and stitch together. Tack the arms to the body right under the neck, see figure A.

Dress

Cut two rectangular pieces of dress fabric in the size of the dress, including seam allowance. Place the pieces right sides together and trace the dress pattern. Stitch up each side, see figure B.

Iron the corners on each side inwards and iron down the seam allowance on the top, see figure C. Reverse and iron the dress.

Put the dress on the figure. Sew along the front and back edges by the neck with the same thread and pull to tighten. Sew and tighten around the bottom edge of the dress, see figure D.

Attach the dress to the body at the bottom by sewing through both the dress and the body.

Fold the fabric for the collar, right sides together, trace from the pattern and sew around the edges. Cut out, reverse and iron the collar. Attach the collar to the figure, see figure E, and fold down.

Make the hair as described on page 12 and the face as described on page 13.

Put glue in the bottom and along the edges of the cup and push the figure down to attach. Tack or glue a hand to her mouth and attach a rose to decorate her hair and wings if you wish.

If you would like the figure to hang, you can tack on a thread for hanging.

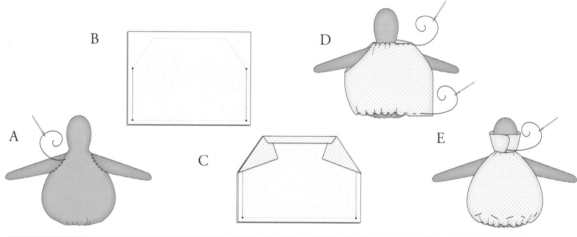

This gorgeous teapot makes a cute pincushion.

Teapots

HOW TO MAKE

Cut a strip of fabric measuring 32 × 16cm (12¾ × 6¼in), including a large seam allowance. Fold the strip right sides together and stitch up the open side. Reverse and iron the seam allowance inwards on the top and bottom.

Tack (baste) along the bottom edge using embroidery yarn. Tighten the bottom and fasten the thread. Cut a small fabric circle and tack it onto the bottom so that the rice or plastic granules will not escape, see figure A. Tack along the top edge. Fill a third of the pot with rice or plastic granules and tightly fill the rest with wadding. Tighten the top and fasten the thread.

Fold the fabric for the spout and handle right sides together, trace the parts from pattern then sew and cut out. Remember to cut notches in the seam allowance where the seam turns inwards.

Reverse the parts, using a thin wooden stick. Use the same technique as turning thin arms and legs, described on page 10, see figure B.

YOU WILL NEED

Fabric for the teapot
Fabric for the teabag
12mm (½in) wadding (batting) ball
Glue
Thread for the teabag
Embroidery yarn
Wadding
Cotton wool
Rice or plastic granules

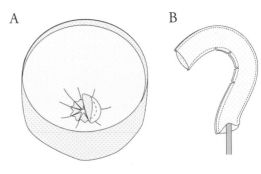

A   B

See pattern on page 144.

Fold the seam allowance inwards and iron the spout and handle. Fill the pieces using a thin wooden stick. Pin the pieces to the teapot, adjust until you are happy with their position then tack to the teapot.

Fold the fabric for the lid right sides together and put a layer of cotton wool beneath the fabric layers. Trace the lid from the pattern, sew and cut out.

Make a little reverse opening through the top layer, reverse and iron. Sew about 5mm (¼in) from the edge around the lid and fill with wadding through the opening.

Place a glass or an object with a radius similar to the seam inside the edge. Put the lid on the glass with the wrong side up and iron on the side that is facing up, using a lot of steam. This technique creates a lid that bulges out on top and is flat underneath, see figure C.

Cut a small fabric circle that just covers the wadding ball with some allowance. Put glue on the ball and attach the fabric with its edges by the hole in the wadding (batting) ball. Push any excess fabric into the hole using a wooden needle, see figure D. Tack the ball to the lid.

Fold the fabric for the teabag right sides together, then trace, sew, cut out, reverse and iron. Tie a knot at the end of some string. Staple the patch and the string together, using a small stapler. The patch and string can also be sewn together if you don't have a suitable stapler.

Glue or tack the lid onto the teapot with the string and patch hanging out, see photo (right).

The teapot can be decorated with a flower ironed on using iron-on interfacing (Vliesofix). The teapot in the photo (far right) is decorated with a patch. The edges are folded in and the patch is tacked on without iron-on interfacing.

C

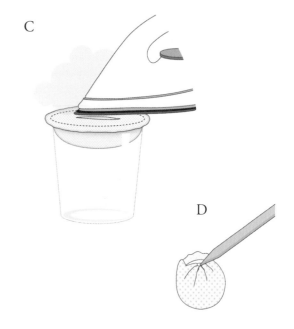

D

In earlier Tilda books you can
find patterns for many food items.
This pie fits the whole picture.
Why not make a café, a store or a
small bakery for a child's room?

Homemade pie

HOW TO MAKE

Cut out a cardboard circle, using the cardboard from the back of a notebook or similar, using the small circle in the pattern. Then cut out a circle in fabric using in the larger size circle from the pattern, adding seam allowance. Fold the seam allowance inwards and sew with embroidery yarn.

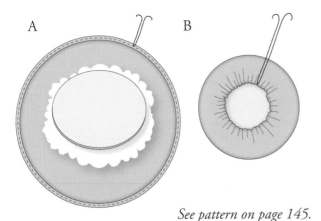

See pattern on page 145.

Place a good amount of wadding (batting) in the middle of the circle and position the cardboard circle on top of the wadding, see figure A. Tighten the fabric circle, see figure B.

It is important to use a lot of wadding to ensure that it doesn't end up on the side of the cardboard when you tighten. The wadding should build all the volume of the pie, as shown in the photo (left).

Notice that the wavy edge is marked with a fold. This means that the pattern should be mirrored on the other side of the fold so that it becomes twice as long.

Fold the fabric right sides together and trace the whole pattern. Sew around, taking care around the waves. Leave a reverse opening in the right side seam.

Cut the wavy edge out; it is very important to cut notches in the seam allowance all the way down to the seam in between each wave. Carefully reverse, making sure to reverse the waves fully with a wooden needle. Iron the wavy edge.

Pin the wavy edge tightly around the pie so that the ends meet. Tack (baste) on the top and bottom with 'invisible' stitches, see figure C.

Fold the fabric for the leaves right sides together then trace the pattern, sew, reverse and iron. Make a seam in the middle of each leaf by hand, then tack every leaf together, see figure D.

Tack or glue the leaves and berries onto the pie.

C

D

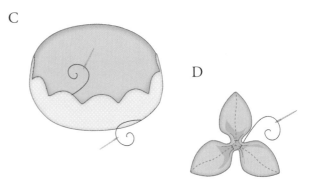

Kitchen ideas

A floral, hand quilted tea cosy or a few small placemats make lovely decorations as well as great gifts. The models are in the book mostly for inspiration – there are countless different patterns for these types of models on the market. Here is a simple description of what to do:

Tea cosy

A tea cosy is made almost entirely like a stocking, see page 26.

Use a large piece of paper, such as wrapping paper or similar, and place it around the teapot. Note the width and height for one side of the tea cosy. Then draw a curved shape well within the measurements to use as pattern.

Stitch up the patches in the front. Cut front, back, and two pieces for the lining all with seam allowances, using the pattern. Attach wadding (batting) to both the front and back.

Quilt the front and back if desired, as described on page 80.

Attach one piece of lining in the front and one in the back. It can be a good idea to draw another pattern after quilting the front and back. Place the two sewn pieces right sides together and sew around. Leave a reverse opening in the lining.

Remove any excess seam allowance, reverse and iron the tea cosy. Push the rest of the lining into the tea cosy and iron. Attach a loop, like the one in Christmas stocking on page 26, or a big bead on the top.

Placemats

Placemats are made in the same way as the lids for teapots on page 53, but without the wadding. Use a circular shape such as a bowl or a lid in the same size as the pattern. The small cups are from a Tilda fabric, ironed on with interfacing (Vliesofix) and then sewn around with buttonhole stitches.

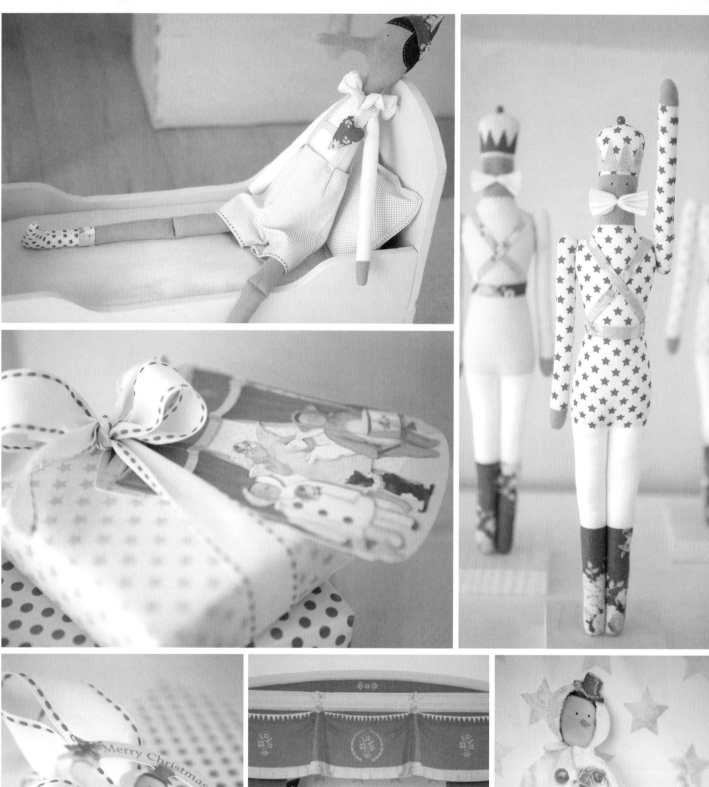

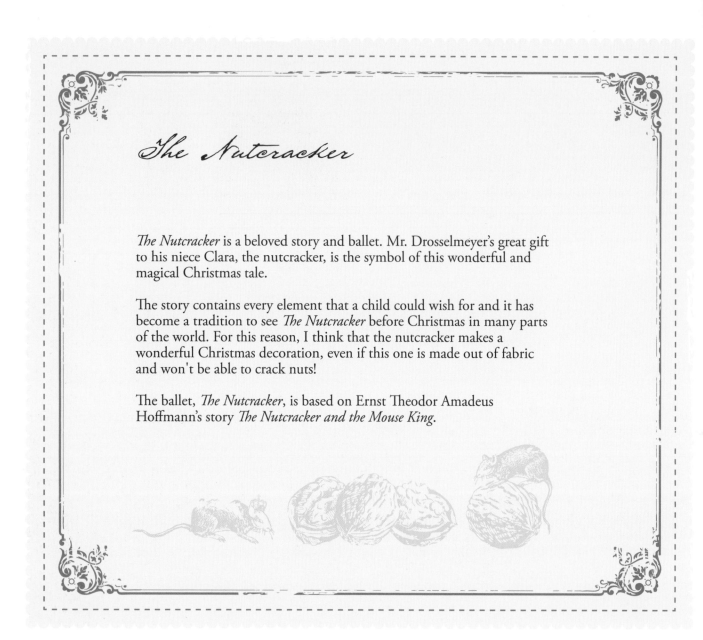

The Nutcracker

The Nutcracker is a beloved story and ballet. Mr. Drosselmeyer's great gift to his niece Clara, the nutcracker, is the symbol of this wonderful and magical Christmas tale.

The story contains every element that a child could wish for and it has become a tradition to see *The Nutcracker* before Christmas in many parts of the world. For this reason, I think that the nutcracker makes a wonderful Christmas decoration, even if this one is made out of fabric and won't be able to crack nuts!

The ballet, *The Nutcracker*, is based on Ernst Theodor Amadeus Hoffmann's story *The Nutcracker and the Mouse King*.

Nutcrackers

HOW TO MAKE

Nutcrackers is made in the same way as the One-legged Tin Soldier on page 39, this time with two legs. The legs are made in one shape, see figure A. After the figure is reversed and ironed, make a seam in between the legs as marked by the dotted line in the pattern, see figure B.

YOU WILL NEED

Fabric for the skin
Fabric for the jacket
and trousers
Fabric for the shoes and hat
Embroidery yarn and beads
to decorate
Materials for the hair, see
page 12
Wadding (batting)

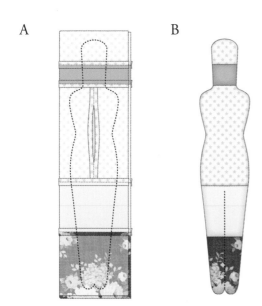

A   B

The triangle shape on the hat is ironed on with interfacing (Vliesofix) and sewn on with buttonhole stitches. The stripes across the chest are sewn using red embroidery yarn and 3mm (⅛in) red beads. The bead on top of the hat is 5mm (¼in).

Moustache
Cut out a piece of fabric measuring 3.5cm (1⅜in) square and make four small pleats. Iron so the pleats remain. Tie a thread around the middle and sew it onto the figure.

See pattern on page 146.

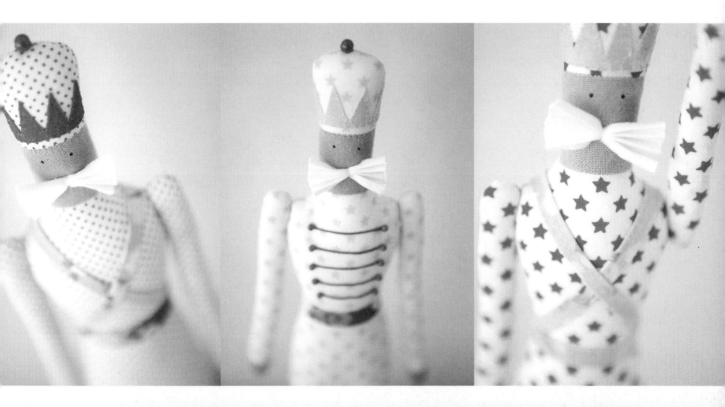

Letters

These letters turned into such a good sofa activity, I ended up making a lot more than originally planned. A tray is handy for sofa crafting!

HOW TO MAKE

I have given patterns for CHRISTMAS, JUL and NOEL in the book. If you want to make different words and letters, enlarge a font and print it out to use as a pattern. You will need to make two of the same letter in cardboard to make one letter.

Carefully cut out two of each letter in cardboard. Start by brushing glue onto one piece of fabric and glue onto the front of one of the letters. Cut out the fabric so that you have about 1cm (⅜in) around the edge and cut notches where there are curves and angles in the letters. Brush glue on the edges and glue to the back of the letter.

When you are ready for the second patch, fold the fabric where it overlaps the first patch. Cut and glue the edges as for the first patch.

Continue until the letter is completely covered with fabric. If you want, you can make a

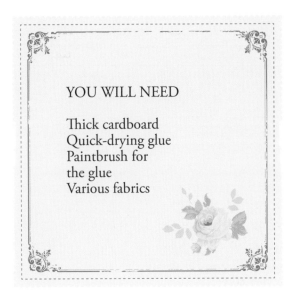

YOU WILL NEED

Thick cardboard
Quick-drying glue
Paintbrush for
the glue
Various fabrics

decorative seam between the different fabrics, see the photo (left).

Glue the other cardboard letter to the back of the fabric covered letter to seal the edges.

The letters can be hung in a string with small clips, and used to hang on a wall or decorate wrapping paper or similar.

See pattern on pages 136, 137, 143 and 147.

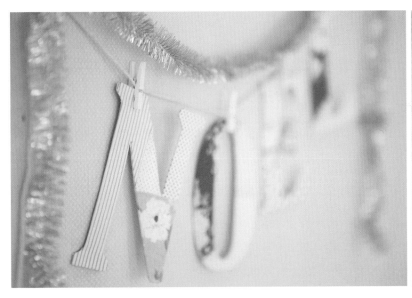

Pinocchio

The story of *Pinocchio* was one of my favorites as a child and it was the Walt Disney version that I knew best. The ragged old magazine was like a treasure under the mattress, along with Bambi, and was taken out and read almost every night. The moral of the story is clear; Pinocchio's nose grows when he's lying, teaching you to listen to your conscience.

There was always something sad about the little wooden figure that wanted more than anything else to become a real boy, but couldn't help but to lie. The figure makes a great instantly-recognizable model for a doll, in fabric this time. And yes, I think he has been lying a little…

Pinocchio's adventures were written by Carlo Collodi for the enjoyment of children around the world. It was first published as an attachment in a children magazine before the stories were collected and published as a book in 1883.

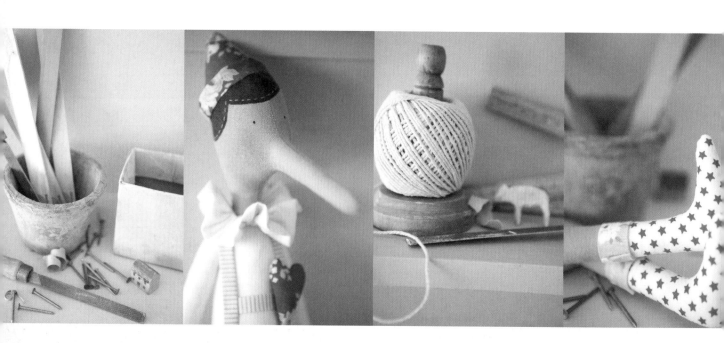

Did you lie, Pinocchio?

Pinocchio doll

HOW TO MAKE

Note that the pattern for the body and legs are divided into pieces to fit the page. Put the pattern back together by positioning point A next to point B.

Body

Cut out a piece of skin-coloured fabric, large enough to fit the head twice in width and a piece of shirt fabric, large enough to fit the body twice, including seam allowances. Sew the shirt piece onto the middle of the head piece and fold the larger piece right sides together. Trace the pattern and sew. Notice the head opening and that the bottom is open with the exception of a small seam on the bottom of each side to attach the fabrics, see figure A.

Cut out the body. Fold the opening in the head and on each side of the bottom opposite so that the seams are over and under each other, and stitch up, see figure B.

Cut notches where the seams turn inwards and release any seam allowance that has caught in the seam where the two fabrics meet.

YOU WILL NEED

Tilda skin fabric
Fabrics for the hat, heart, shirt, dungarees, shoes and the edge of the shoes
Buttons for the dungarees
Embroidery yarn
Materials for the hair, see page 12
Wadding (batting)

Reverse the body using a wooden needle and iron. Fill with wadding (batting) and stitch up the bottom.

See pattern on pages 148–149.

A   B

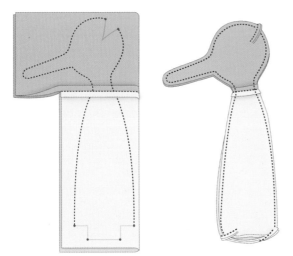

Legs and arms

Stitch up the fabrics for the legs and arms in the same way as for the body. Fold the attached pieces right sides together, trace, sew and cut out. Leave a small reverse opening in both legs and the arms through the fabric marked in the pattern then reverse the arms and legs.

Iron the pieces and fill with wadding before you stitch up the reverse opening. Fill the legs up to the dotted lines and make a seam for the knees, see figure C, before filling the rest of the leg. Tack (baste) the reverse opening closed.

Attach the legs and arms tightly to the body by sewing through the whole doll with embroidery yarn and a needle, see figure D.

Paint the hair as described on page 12 and make a face as described on page 13. Make a small seam by hand at the hairline if desired, see the photo (below).

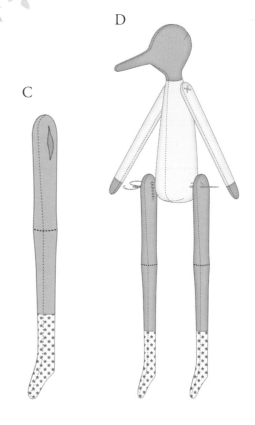

D

C

Dungarees

Cut out two pieces for the shorts. Note that the pattern is marked with a fold so the fabric should be doubled. Place the pieces right sides together and stitch up both sides, see figure E.

Fold the shorts the other way so that the seam is over and under each other, and stitch up the legs, see figure F.

Reverse the shorts and iron the seam allowance inwards. Attach the seam allowance to the leg opening with a decorative seam. Here the seam is made by hand with red embroidery yarn.

Cut two strips measuring 22 × 3.5cm (8½ × 1⅜in) for the braces and one strip measuring 5 × 3.5cm (2 × 1⅜in) for the middle part, seam allowance included. Fold inwards by 6–7mm (¼in) on one of the short sides on each of the long strips to hide the edges. Fold inwards by 7mm (¼in) along the long sides of all the strips, fold and iron the strips in half so they have a width of 1cm (⅜in). Tack or use a sewing machine to stitch up the open sides.

Put the shorts on the figure. Make two tucks in the front and two in the back then pin and sew.

Attach the neat end of the two long strips in the front by attaching with buttons. Cross the strips over at the back and attach the braces inside the shorts. Attach the small strip under the braces in the front, see figure G.

Hat

Fold the fabric for the hat right sides together, trace the hat from the pattern and sew. Cut out, reverse and iron.

Fold and iron the area below the dotted line in the pattern inwards, see figure H. Fold and iron approximately 1.5cm (⅝in) of the edge upwards, see figure I. Sew the hat to the head, see figure J.

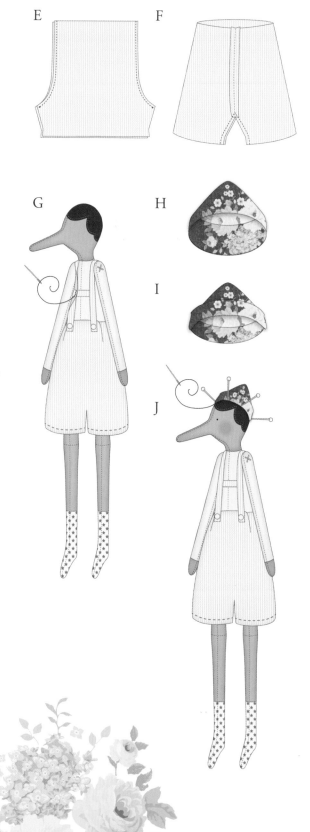

E   F

G   H

I

J

Cut a strip measuring 35 × 5cm (14 × 2in) for the collar, adding some seam allowance. Stitch up the two short ends. Fold the seam allowance inwards along the sides and fold the strips in half so that they become about 2.5cm (1in) in height. Tack along the open edge, pull the collar over the head, tighten and attach, see figure K.

Cut two strips measuring 7 × 2cm (2¾ × ¾in) for the edges of the shoes, adding seam allowance. Fold the seam allowance inwards along each side and tack it onto the leg above the transition between skin and shoe fabric.

Heart
Fold the fabric for the little heart right sides together, trace and sew. Cut the heart out and make a reverse opening through one fabric layer, see figure L.

Reverse, iron and fill the heart then tack closed the reverse opening. Tack the heart to the figure.

K   L

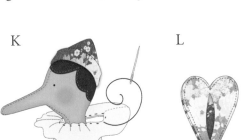

Stuffed stockings

YOU WILL NEED

Various fabrics for the
patches and loop
Fabric for lining
Wadding (batting)

HOW TO MAKE

Add 30cm (12in) to the top of the pattern for the
Christmas stocking so that length of the whole
stocking is approximately 65cm (26in).

Sew patches together until you have a piece that is
big enough for the stocking twice. Place a piece of
wadding (batting) in the same size underneath, see
figure A.

See pattern on page 151.

A

You can usually place a piece of fabric in the back and quilt normally, however you may find that the fabric is too thick with the lining in place. I would recommend quilting through the patched fabric and the wadding only. On this stocking, I quilted at the end but it became more difficult as I reached the bottom part.

Attach a corresponding piece of lining to the top of the stocking, see figure B. Fold the stocking right sides together, trace the pattern and sew. Leave a reverse opening in the lining, see figure C.

Cut, reverse and iron the stocking, push the lining into it and iron down the edge.

Attach a loop in the same way as for the Ballerina Christmas Stocking on page 26.

B

C

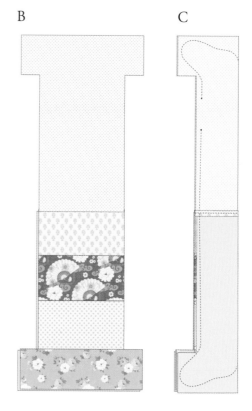

Hand quilting

It has to be said that I am no expert at quilting, either with a sewing machine or by hand. Maybe that's why I like the rough expression of the hand quilt, as it is difficult to get it wrong. Something about this technique reminds me of the old rugs that Grandma left in the cottage that have been washed several times, shrunken and dried into the wrong position.

Ideally you will have the front, the soft layer of cotton wool and the back, however some of the models are only quilted through the front and the wadding because of the lining. When you pull the thread you will still achieve an effect. To prevent your quilt from shrinking, you must remember to use a large seam allowance.

To attach the different layers I've used a tacking (basting) gun that can be bought in quilting stores. The tacking gun shoots small plastic clips through all the layers to keep everything together while you quilt.

The models to the right have streaks right across with approximately 1–1.5cm (⅜–⅝in) in between. The stitches should be a maximum of 2–3mm (⅛in) on top and 1–1.5cm (⅜–⅝in) long underneath. Every time you get to the edge, pull the thread a little to create some wrinkles and spread them out evenly. You don't have to pull much to create a nice effect.

Make a couple of stitches to secure the thread before you continue. It is a good idea to try and pull about the same amount every time and iron when you have finished to secure the wrinkles. For the patched stocking on page 79, I have quilted on top of the pattern of the fabric, see the photo on page 78.

Bambi

As for most children, it was through Walt Disney that I first got to know Bambi, however the story was originally written by Felix Salten in 1923. Felix was Jewish and his stories were therefore banned by Hitler in 1936. The story of Bambi still managed to live on and was made known to the whole world by the Walt Disney movie, based on the book.

Bambi is one of the saddest and strongest stories from my childhood. The fear of losing your mother is significant among any child, but as in most fairy tales, this time the story also ended in a happily ever after.

Deer

HOW TO MAKE

Body
Fold the fabric for the body and legs right sides together and trace one body, two back legs and two front legs from the pattern.

Sew around the different parts. Note that there is an opening for the head and in the back, in addition to the reverse opening on the body.

Cut out the parts. Fold the opening in the head and in the back opposite, so that the seams are over and under each other and stitch up, see figure A. Reverse and iron the body.

Cut a reverse opening through one layer of the fabric, as marked in the leg pattern. Make sure you cut the reverse opening on opposite sides on each of the legs so that you create left and right legs, see figure B. Reverse and iron the legs.

Fill the body tightly with wadding (batting) and stitch up the opening.

It is important to fill the slimmest part of the leg tightly and evenly to allow the deer to stand up straightly. Use a wooden needle and push the wadding evenly down a little at the time. If the leg 'cracks', take the wadding out and start again. Stitch up the opening.

YOU WILL NEED

Fabric for the body
Lining for the ears
Insert wadding (batting)
Embroidery yarn
Wadding
Sticks for the antlers
Ribbon and fabric
to decorate

See pattern on pages 150–151.

A

B

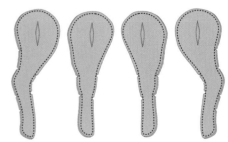

Pin the legs on to the body and make sure that the deer can stand evenly. On these figures, the legs are firstly attached using a glue gun then they are pushed tightly against the body. The thighs are sewn around using small stitches. This makes the legs look nice and solid.

Instead of using a glue gun, you can tack the legs onto the body using embroidery yarn, but I still recommend that you stitch around the thighs so that they will be tightly attached to the body.

To remember the exact location for the legs, you can draw around the thigh with a vanishing fabric marker before you remove the pins.

Snout
To create a nice looking snout, firstly make a stitch to squeeze it flat, see figure C. Draw the outline with a vanishing marker pen before filling with embroidery yarn, see figure D.

Ears
Lay out the skin fabric and lining fabric right sides together with the wadding underneath.

Trace, sew around, cut out and reverse. Fold the seam allowance inwards and iron the ears. Fold the ears in half and make a couple of stitches to keep them in place, see figure E. Tack the ears onto the figure, see figure F.

Twist a small scissor point into the head in front of the ears where the antlers should be positioned, see photo (right). Place some glue at the end of the sticks to be used for the antlers and twist into the holes.

Make a face, as described on page 13. Tie a ribbon around the neck of the deer and decorate with flowers, see page 120.

C   D

E   F

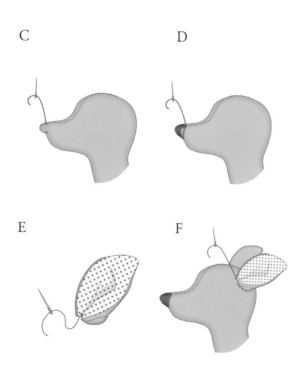

Mushroom

The mushrooms do not stand by themselves; they are glued onto a surface. Glue them onto a piece of wood or a rock using a glue gun or use a Tilda figure stand to make them stand.

To make the description of the project pieces easy to understand, we use the terms red and white fabric, however you can of course use fabrics in different colours if you prefer.

HOW TO MAKE

Cut one circle in red and one in white fabric, using the pattern. Cut a strip of white fabric measuring 6 × 42cm (2½ × 16½in) for the large mushroom and 5 × 36cm (2 × 14¼in) for the smaller mushroom. Add seam allowances.

Sew the two short ends of the strip together, fold down the edges and tack (baste) around using embroidery yarn, see figure A.

Tighten the yarn so that the strip become the same size as the other circles. Tie a bow in embroidery yarn so it can easily be untied it, see figure B.

See pattern on page 152.

A

B

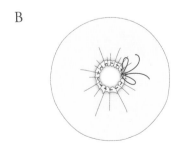

Lay out the pieces with the white circle on the bottom, the red circle in the middle and the tightened circle on top with the wrong side up, see figure C.

Stitch up the three layers, see figure D. Reverse the tightened edge so that the red fabric is turned out on one side and the right side of the tightened circle is on the other.

The white fabric in the middle is there to give the mushroom a better shape when it is filled. Make an opening in the middle of the white fabric for filling, see figure E. Fill through the opening so that the wadding (batting) is between the white fabric in the middle and the red fabric.

Fold the fabric for the stem right sides together, trace, sew around, cut out, reverse, iron and fill. Place the stem at the reverse opening and tighten firmly around it. Pull the edge down a little and tack a few stitches, see figure F.

Cut a strip measuring approximately 3.5 × 35cm (1⅜ × 14in) for the large mushroom and 3 × 30cm (1¼ × 12in) for the small mushroom, adding seam allowance. Sew the two short ends together and fold the seam allowance inwards on every long side. Fold the strip in half and tack along the open side, see figure G. Tighten the strip around the mushroom and tack it onto the stem, see figure H.

C

D

E

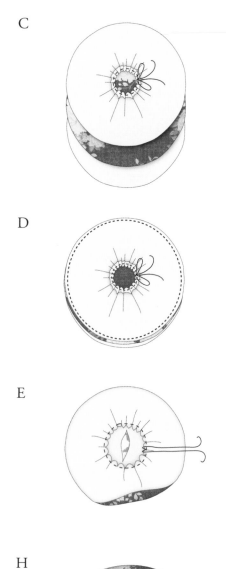

F

G

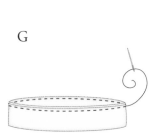

H

Fox boy

Bear girl

Hare girl

Deer girl

Hare boy

Fox girl

Miniature animals

When I was a child, I thought there were little creatures that lived in nooks and crannies, hidden from humans. If I spent a lot of time somewhere, I made sure to make a little house in connection with an outside wall or a flight of stairs. I made comfortable beds from cotton wool and old boxes, rugs from blankets and small bowls from hazelnut tops. I enjoyed this little game so much that it didn't really matter if the creatures really existed.

I think a lot of children are fascinated by small figures; they are easy to play with and evoke adventures in the imagination. For adults, they are great to use for Christmas and Easter decorations.

Using the same basic pattern, here you can make a large variety of small figures. Read more about miniatures on page 11.

HOW TO MAKE

Sew a strip of skin fabric and a strip of clothing fabric together. Fold the finished strips right sides together. Trace the pattern so that the transition between the two fabrics is on the dotted line on the pattern and sew around, see figure A.

YOU WILL NEED

Various fabrics for the patches and loop
Fabric for the lining
Insert wadding (batting)

See pattern on page 153.

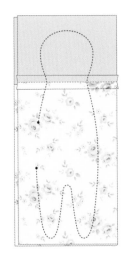

Fold the fabric for the arms, collar, ears and snout in half. Trace the parts you will need for the animal you are making from the pattern. Sew around, cut out and reverse the parts. Add in the seam allowance by the openings of arms, ears and snout. Iron all the parts using the tip of the iron.

Fill the arms and tack (baste) them onto each side of the body, see figure B.

Make a ball of wadding (batting) and push it into the snout. Pin the snout to the face then tack, see figure C. Embroider a small snout.

Attach the ears as shown in the photographs. Attach the little collar around the neck with a few stitches.

Skirt

Cut a strip measuring 3 × 25cm (1¼ x 10in), only adding seam allowance on one of the long sides as well as the short sides. Stitch up the two short sides, fold the seam allowance inwards and iron the skirt.

Tack along the folded edge and tighten the skirt around the waist. Attach with a few stitches.

Shorts

Stitch up the shorts in the same way as Pinocchio's dungaree shorts on page 76.

Antlers

Small branches are used as antlers for the deer. Attach the antlers in the same way as for the deer on page 86.

Make the face as described on page 13.

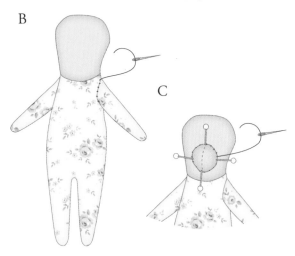

B

C

Best friends

Decorating the tree

Miniature animals are
nice to use as motifs in
bell jars. Here is a
small seamstress bunny.

Theatre

There are many ways that you can make a small theatre.

The paper theatre is made from Tilda paper with theatre theme but you can also make your own curtains from ordinary paper and cardboard. A small cardboard box is glued to the back for support and the stage is made from cardboard and sheets of paper with a plank pattern.

Iron interfacing (Vliesofix) to some fabric to make the small flag garland. The flags are folded in half, cut out around a string and glued together by ironing over them.

The grey theatre is simply a stool with curtains attached under it.

A little nervous for today's performance...

On page 153 you can find the pattern for small Christmas baskets.

When cutting out the basket, you might want to use decorative scissors for the top edges. Mark the fold (marked with a dotted line in the pattern) with a ruler and something sharp before you fold. Glue the basket together and attach a strip for hanging.

The ornaments are made from tissue paper folded into an accordion shape. Tie a string to the middle and pull out the edges to form a circle. Finally use some glue to attach the edges.

 *Princesses*

You can't deny the importance of princesses when you enter the world of fairy tales. Some are sensitive, others are smart, they usually come with a kingdom, and then the question is usually who deserves them.

To be a princess is about style, class and about seeing your own values. It might also be about being spoiled because it is difficult to be a princess if no one treats you like one. I hope we all get the opportunity to be princesses once in a while.

On page 110 you can find instructions for making a nightgown; here are the instructions for a princess with a dress.

YOU WILL NEED

Tilda skin fabric
Various fabrics for the legs, dress, and crown
Wadding (batting)
Materials for the hair, see page 12.

HOW TO MAKE

Make a doll in the same way as the Ballerinas on page 19, this time making the legs out of one fabric instead of two. Attach a ribbon around the chest to decorate before attaching the arms.

See pattern for the body and crown on pages 138–139.

Dress

Cut out a piece of fabric measuring 25 × 54cm (10 × 21¾in), including seam allowance. Sew the two short edges together to make the skirt 25cm (10in) in height and 27cm (10¾in) in width.

Fold and iron the seam allowance inwards on the top and bottom and attach the seam allowance with some stitches at the bottom.

Reverse the skirt and tack (baste) around the edge on top. Tighten the skirt around the waist and attach it with some stitches.

Crown

Fold the fabric for the crown right sides together and trace the crown pattern. Sew a small seam measuring 1–1.5mm (¹⁄₁₆in). Be careful and stop every time you get to a corner. Put the needle down and turn the fabric before you continue. Cut out with as little as 2–3mm (⅛in) seam allowance. Cut notches into the seam between every point on the crown, see figure A.

Reverse the crown carefully using a sharp wooden needle. Sand the tip of the needle first so it won't go through the fabric. Iron the crown and stitch up the small opening. Form a circle and stitch up the two ends, see figure B.

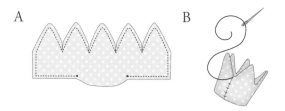

A   B

The Princess and the Pea

The Princess and the Pea is one of the most popular princess tales. Imagine being so delicate as to be bothered by a pea several mattresses down…

The tale is so fun to reproduce with a doll, a pile of fabric mattresses, a little green bead to represent the pea and a cup to represent the pot. An old quilted pillowcase has been used as the blanket. A royal atmosphere has been created by adding the crown on the top with curtains hanging down.

The Princess and the Pea is said to have originated from Swedish folk tale tradition, which Hans Christian Andersen heard as a child. He published his own version in 1835.

This little princess is elegantly posing for the camera...

Nightgown princesses

Princesses in nightgowns are essential when recreating The Princess and the Pea. These princesses wear long stockings with a ruffle edge and, of course, they sleep with their gowns on.

HOW TO MAKE

Make the body same as the Ballerinas on page 19, this time without the waist.

The legs are made from two strips of fabric in the same ways as for the Ballerinas, however the transition between the patterns should this time be by the top dotted line on the pattern.

Ruffle edge
Cut a strip of fabric measuring 25 × 4cm (10 × 1¾in) including seam allowance. Fold approximately 11–12mm (½in) along each long side so that the folded edges barely overlap each other in the middle. Tack (baste) down along the middle through all three layers, see figure A.

Attach the ruffle in the transition between the skin fabric and the stocking fabric. Fold the edges inwards at the back and tack together, see figure B.

See pattern for the nightgown on page 139.

A

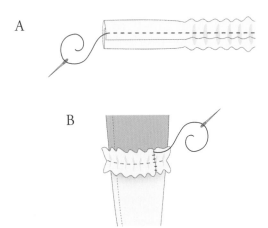

B

Nightgown

Cut out two nightgown shapes from the pattern, including seam allowance. Cut a strip measuring 55 × 5cm (22 × 2in) for the ruffle, including seam allowance.

Cut out two sleeves from the pattern and add seam allowance. Iron the long sides of the sleeves inwards. Stitch up one side of the sleeve to one dress piece, see figure C, then stitch up the other side to the other dress piece. Repeat with the other sleeve so that the dress is attached through the sleeves, see figure D.

Fold the dress right sides together and stitch up one side. Reverse the dress.

Iron the seam allowance from one long side inwards for the ruffle, and stitch it to the dress. Sew a 6mm (¼in) seam with a sewing machine along the other long side without attaching the

thread. Pull the thread until the length of the ruffle is the same length as the dress.

Lay out the ruffle and dress right sides together and stitch up, see figure C. Iron down the ruffle. Fold the dress right sides together and stitch up the open side. Reverse and iron the dress.

Tack along the neck, put the dress on the doll and tighten. Attach the thread. Sew and tighten the openings on the sleeves.

Tack from right under the sleeve, around the chest and back and tighten the dress around the chest, see the photo (right).

Sew a crown as described on page 104.

C

D

E
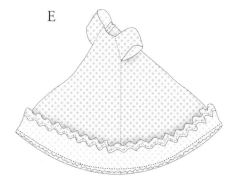

THE MATTRESSES AND PILLOW

The princess' blanket is an old quilted pillowcase. The mattresses have to be sewn from the measurements of the doll bed you are using. If you want corners to add volume you can add e.g. 1.5cm (⅝in) on each side.

When you have sewn around, fold each corner opposite so that the seams are over and under each other. Then make a seam across, approximately 1.5cm (⅝in) from the edge. Remember to include a reverse opening. Reverse, iron and fill the mattress.

You can use Velcro to make the mattresses lay nicely on top of each other.

The pillow is made from a piece of fabric measuring 20 × 30cm (8 × 12in), adding seam allowance. Fold the fabric right sides together to make the pillow approximately 20 × 15cm (8 × 6in).

Stitch up the open sides, leaving a reverse opening in one of the long sides. Reverse and iron.

Make a seam approximately 1cm (⅜in) inside the edge, leaving the reverse opening also in the seam right above the other opening.

Fill the pillow, stitch up the top opening with a sewing machine and stitch the bottom opening by hand.

Princess and the Pea hanging rug

HOW TO MAKE

Cut out two pieces of fabric measuring 85 × 33cm (34 × 13¼in) and a piece of insert wadding (batting) measuring 83 × 33cm (33¼ × 13¼in) for the back, adding seam allowance.

Lay out the pieces right sides together and place the wadding underneath the fabrics so that it lies against the fabrics on the bottom. Pin the pieces together and sew around the edges. Leave the top open, see figure A. Remove any excess seam allowance along the stitched up sides.

Reverse and iron the rug. Iron the part of the top without wadding inwards and fold it down by 3cm (1¼in) so it becomes approximately 80cm (32in) in height. Iron to mark the edges to get an idea of the finished size of the rug.

When complete, fold the edges around a hanger and tack. The area without wadding is easier to use.

YOU WILL NEED

Skin fabric
Fabrics for the nightgown, crown and stockings
Fabric for the rug
Various fabrics for the mattresses
Fabrics for the bed and pot
Fabrics for the blanket and pillow
Insert wadding (batting)
Wadding
Hanger or similar

A

See pattern on page 154.

Bed
Cut a strip measuring 20 × 2.5cm (8 × 1in), and two strips measuring 15 × 0.7cm (6 × ¼in) for the bed, adding seam allowance.

Iron the seam allowance inwards along the long sides on all the pieces and the short sides on the thin strips. Place the bed on the middle of the rug about 10cm (4in) from the bottom edge, see the photo (left). Attach with pins.

Mattresses
In the pattern you will find mattresses in three different sizes. On this rug, I have used five large, five medium and five small mattresses.

Fold the fabric right sides together, trace and sew around. Cut out, make a reverse opening through one fabric layer and reverse. Iron the mattress to highlight the corners.

Much of the charm in this rug lies in the wrinkly mattresses that give life and texture to it. Leave the mattresses in water for a few minutes and knead each one into a small ball, one at a time. Unfold the mattresses and let them dry flat. When the mattresses are dry, fill them with wadding (batting), using a wooden needle. Stitch up the reverse opening.

Sew the mattresses together by hand one at a time, see figure B. If you want to give the rug more life, don't make the mattress stack completely straight, see photo on page 112. Pin the 'mattress strip' to the rug.

Blanket and pillow
Fold the fabric for the blanket and pillow in half, make a rectangle measuring 13 × 9cm (6¼ × 3⅝in) for the pillow and trace the blanket from the pattern.

B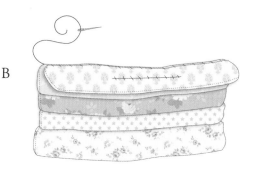

Sew around, cut out the pieces and make a reverse opening through one layer of fabric. Reverse and iron. Fill the blanket and pillow and stitch up the opening.

Cut a strip measuring 80 × 3cm (30 × 1¼in) for a ruffle for the pillow and a strip measuring 65 × 3cm (26 × 1¼in) for the blanket. Seam allowance is included. Iron the strips in half to a width of 1.5cm (⅝in). Make a 6mm (¼in) seam of along the open side of each strip.

Pull the thread so that the strip is the same length as two short sides and one long side for the pillow. Pin the ruffle to the pillow and tack from the top, see figure C. Make the ruffle for the blanket in the same way and attach, see figure D.

Quilt approximately 5mm (¼in) from the edge of the pillow and by the edge where the ruffle is attached to the blanket. Pull the thread for some extra effect and attach. Also sew along the seam on the edge without ruffles on the blanket and pull. Attach the thread.

Lay out all the pieces and pin them to the rug as desired. Start by tacking the bed, mattresses and pillow. Leave an opening on the top of the mattresses so you can place the princess, see photo (right). The blanket is attached to the mattresses.

A small cup from a Tilda fabric can be ironed on as a pot. A decorative flower from page 120 is used to embellish the pillow.

Quilt around the edge of the whole rug, see the photo (right). The simple markings are made with a vanishing fabric marker and quilted. Fold the top edge around a hanger and tack.

Place the princess between the mattresses/ blanket and rug. Sew a seam between the two mattresses as a stopper so the princess doesn't fall down to the bottom.

LITTLE PRINCESS

The Little Princess is almost the same as the Little Ballerina on page 35, however this time both arms and legs are attached downwards. The pattern is on page 154. The legs are made with two strips of fabric, so that the transition between the two fabrics is by the dotted line.

When all the parts are sewn, reversed and filled, the seam allowance by the openings for the body and arms should be folded inwards. Put the legs inside the opening for the body and attach the arms to the body, see figure E. Attach the nightgown and the crown as shown in the Nightgown Princess on page 109.

C

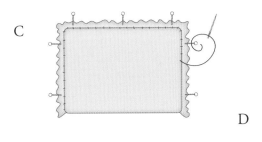

D

E

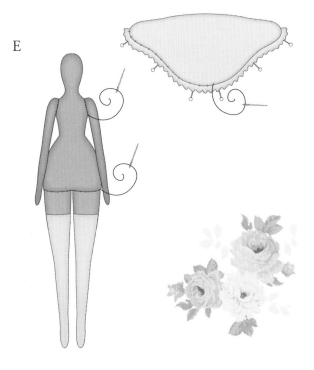

Princess Make-up Bag

These make-up bags are only about 10cm (4in) in height when they completed and might therefore not be able to be used as a make-up bag for anybody other than small princesses! For the rest of us, they can be used to hold coins. If you want a make-up bag that fits more inside, you can easily multiply the pattern to make it larger.

HOW TO MAKE

Cut out two pieces of fabric measuring 18 × 8.5cm (7¼ × 3½in) and two of the same size for lining, adding seam allowance. Cut two pieces of fabric measuring 12 × 8cm (4¾ × 3¼in), adding seam allowance.

Cut a strip measuring 6 × 2cm (2⅜ × ¾in) for the loop, adding seam allowance. Iron the seam allowance inwards along the long sides then iron the strip in half. Stitch up the open side.

Sew a 6mm (¼in) seam along one of the long sides on each of the 18 × 8.5cm (7¼ × 3½in) pieces, without attaching the thread. Pull the thread until the length of the edge is 12cm (½in). Sew one piece of fabric and one piece of lining onto each of the sides of the strips measuring 12 × 8cm (4¾ × 3¼in), see figure A.

Fold and iron each piece in half, wrong sides together, and sew one piece on each side of the zip, see figure B.

YOU WILL NEED

Fabric for the bag
Fabric for the lining
Fabric for the flowers
Zip

Fold opposite so that fabric and fabric and lining and lining are right sides together. Fold the loop double and place it in between the layers in the edge, on the side where the fabrics are sewn together.

Stitch up each side so that the zip and the loop are attached. Open the zip and stitch up the rest, except for a reverse opening in the lining, see figure C.

A   B   C

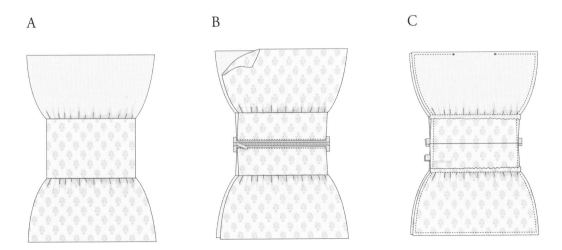

Fold each corner of the fabric and lining opposite, so that the seams are over and under each other. Measure approximately 1.5cm (⅝in) from the seam on the edge and make a seam across. Cut off the corner outside of the seam, see figure D.

Cut off any excess seam allowance as well as the edges of the zip and the loop. Reverse the bag and push the lining into the fabric.

To attach the loose ends of the zip while making the zip a little lower down into the bag, make a fold where the edge of the zip ends. Turn the fold up so that the zip turns down. You may have to adjust the corners little to make them look neat, as the edges of the zip are already attached.

Tack a seam 3–4 mm (⅛in) down from the new fold through the fabric and zip edge, see figure E.

D

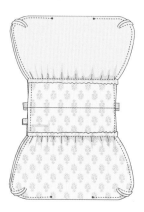

E

DECORATIVE FLOWERS

Decorative flowers are made from strips of fabric. The large flowers are made from strips approximately 3cm (1¼in) wide and the small flowers from strips approximately 2cm (¾in) wide. The length varies between fabrics; you would need to do some trial and error. You do not need seam allowance for the strips. When you attach them to a model, the running edge will not be visible.

If you want, you can cut a strip from the whole length of the fabric. Fold the end and fold the strip along the long side, wrong sides together. Hold the strip together as you sew. Begin by tacking a little, tightening to make the ruffles and start shaping the rosette like the flowers in the photos.

When you are happy with the size, simply cut off the edge, push it underneath the flower and attach it all together.

Put some lavender in the hearts for a wonderful scent.

Nightshirt hearts

HOW TO MAKE

Cut a strip of fabric measuring 16.5 × 13cm (6⅜ × 5in) and another measuring 5.5 × 13cm (2¼ × 5in), adding seam allowance. Stitch up the two strips, leaving an opening of about 5cm (2in) in the seam, see figure A.

Mark the middle by folding the strip in half and ironing the fold. Fold each end to the middle, mark the middle again and iron. Unfold the strip with the front side facing upwards.

Cut a strip measuring 1.2 × 13cm (½ × 5in), adding seam allowance. Iron the seam allowance inwards on each long side. Place the strip towards the middle of the half without the reverse opening and place the patch underneath the strip. Use the heart pattern to ensure the patch is not placed outside the heart. Attach the edge, see figure B.

Fold the fabric piece right sides together, trace the pattern and sew. Cut out the heart, reverse, iron and fill. Stitch up the reverse opening. Attach the buttons and the string for hanging.

YOU WILL NEED

Fabric for the heart
Patch from an old
piece of clothing
or a logo
Small buttons
Wadding (batting)

See pattern on page 146.

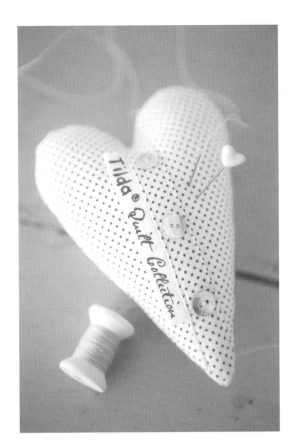

A

B

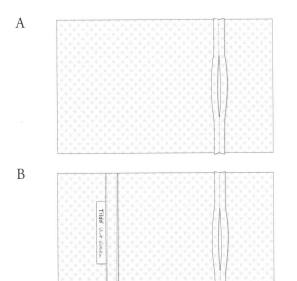

The Fox's Widow

In some fairy tales there are certain memorable parts that really make children think and one of these parts is from the fairy tale *The Fox's Widow*.

"Once upon a time there was a fox and the fox's wife that lived in a happy marriage. Sometimes marriages are like that. But one day when the fox had been out stealing hens from the farmer, he ate so many he got sick and died. The wife cried and mourned but he didn't come back to life."

I always imagine the mourning fox's widow surrounded by hen angels.

The Fox's Widow is from Asbjørnsen and Moe's collection of Norwegian folktales, published in 1941. The puppet film *The Fox's Widow* by Ivo Caprino was released in 1962.

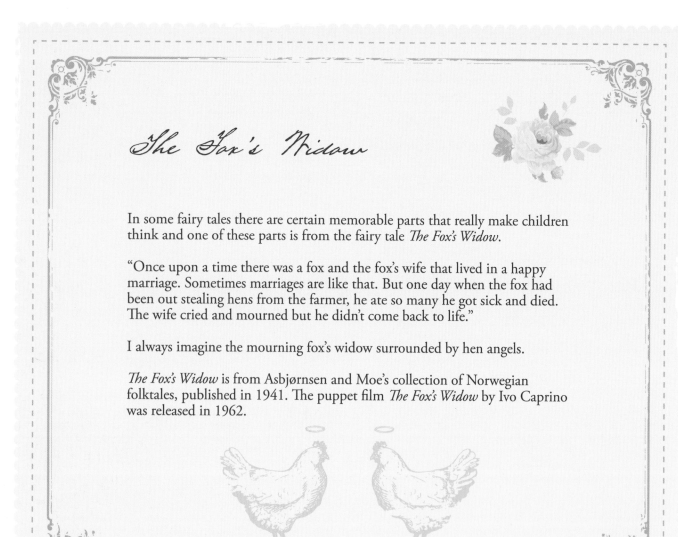

Foxes

HOW TO MAKE

Notice that the pattern for the body and legs for the large and medium fox is split up to fit the page. Lay out the pieces so that A and B are placed next to each other.

Fold the fabric for the body right sides together and trace one body, two arms, two legs and two ears from the pattern.

Sew around all the pieces. Note the opening on the head and that the bottom is open with the exception of a small seam on the bottom of each side, mostly to attach the fabrics.

See pattern on pages 155–159.

Cut out all the pieces. Fold the opening in the head and on each side of the bottom of the body opposite, so that the seams are under and over each other. Stitch up, see figure A.

Make a small reverse opening for the legs and arms through one fabric layer, as marked in the pattern. Reverse, iron and fill all the parts. Stitch up the reverse openings.

Attach the legs and arms tightly to the body by sewing straight through with embroidery yarn and a long needle, see figure B.

Fold the seam allowance by the ear openings inwards. Fill each ear with a little wadding (batting), fold them a little and pin before sewing, see the photo (right).

Sew the snout the same way as described for the deer on page 85 and make the face as described on page 13.

The fox's dress is made the same way as the Nightgown Princesses' dress on page 109.

The edge for the large dress should measure 60 × 5cm (24 × 2in), the edge for the medium dress should measure 50 × 4.5cm (20 × 1¾in) and the edge for the small dress should measure 40 × 3.5cm (16 × 1⅜in).

Decorative flowers from page 120 are nice to use to embellish the dresses.

A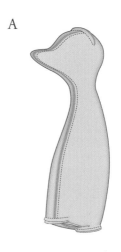

B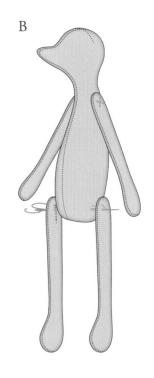

Angel Hens

HOW TO MAKE

Fold the fabric for the body right sides together and trace one body and two wings from the pattern. Sew around and cut out the body and wings.

Note that the opening in the body should be cut out like a triangle. Fold and iron the seam allowance around the opening inwards. Fill the body and push the two tips by the opening together. Stitch up the opening, see figure A.

Make a small reverse opening through one layer of fabric on each wing. Note that they should be on opposite sides to create one left and one right wing. Reverse, iron and fill the wings.

Cut two strips measuring 11 × 3cm (4¼ × 1¼in) for the thighs, adding seam allowance. Stitch up the two short sides, reverse and iron the seam allowance inwards on both sides.

Tack (baste) one side of the thigh to the hen, see the photo (left). Tack around the other edge, fill with wadding (batting) and a small stick and tighten around the stick. If the stick will not stay in place, use a little glue. Repeat with the other thigh.

Tack the wings onto the body, glue the wooden tip for beak in place and make a face as described on page 13.

Push a wire halo into the head of the angel hen and attach string for hanging.

A

See pattern on page 143.

YOU WILL NEED

Fabric for the body
Tip of a wooden stick
Wire for the halo
Sticks for the legs
Wadding (batting)

It is nice to decorate a girl's room with angels. Here are some angel ideas to inspire you.

You can find more about Christmas baskets and ornaments on page 98.

Birdcages, ribbons, paper, decorations and the wooden boxes are all from the Tilda range.

Acknowledgments

SØLVI DOS SANTOS

Photographer Sølvi Dos Santos' work has been very popular in the past. She has an unusual talent of capturing light and motifs in the right environment and has become known around the world for her beautiful interior books.

INGRID SKAANSAR

Ingrid Skaansar has a long history as a stylist and as a product developer for Sia. She has also worked with Tilda for eleven years and her ability to create the right environment and keep the project on track is highly valued.

We have more fun with each project we work on and I am already looking forward to the next!

TOM UNDHJEM

Tom runs Undhjem Media and has a lot of experience with image processing and graphical services. He has become indispensable for the progress of the Tilda books and always walks the extra mile to make sure everything works properly.

CECILIE FISKE LARSEN

Cecilie is the model in the book and acts as the young mother in the house perfectly. Discovered through acquaintances and with little modelling experience, she has a great attitude and much patience.

Also, thanks to CAPPELEN DAMM that has had to work hard to get this book completed.

Suppliers

UK

Stitch Craft Create
Brunel House, Forde Close,
Newton Abbot, Devon,
TQ12 4PU
www.stitchcraftcreate.co.uk

Panduro Hobby
Westway House, Transport
Avenue, Brentford, Middlesex,
TW8 9HF
www.pandurohobby.co.uk

**Coast and Country
Crafts & Quilts**
Cornish Garden Nurseries,
Barras Moor, Perranarworthal,
Nr Truro, Cornwall, TR3 7PE
www.coastandcountry
crafts.co.uk

Fred Aldous Ltd.
37 Lever Street,
Manchester, M1 1LW
www.fredaldous.co.uk

The Fat Quarters
5 Choprell Road, Blackhall Mill,
Newcastle, NE17 7TN
www.thefatquarters.co.uk

The Sewing Bee
52 Hillfoot Street, Dunoon,
Argyll, PA23 7DT
www.thesewingbee.co.uk

Threads and Patches
48 Aylesbury Street,
Fenny Stratford, Bletchley,
Milton Keynes, MK2 2BU
www.threadsandpatches.co.uk

USA

Coats and Clark USA
PO Box 12229,
Greenville, SC29612-0229
www.coatsandclark.com

Connecting Threads
13118 NE 4th Street,
Vancouver, WA 9884
www.connectingthreads.com

Hamels Fabrics
5843 Lickman Road,
Chilliwack, British Columbia,
V2R 4B5
www.hamelsfabrics.com

Keepsake Quilting
Box 1618 Center Harbor,
NH 03226
www.keepsakequilting.com

Props

It is thanks to the nice interior and clothing boutiques in Tønsberg that we have a constant inflow of props for Tilda's world.

This time the following boutiques were used:

NOA NOA has contributed with clothes.
Sandefjord, phone: + 47 33 46 00 90
Tønsberg, phone: + 47 33 31 99 00

LANDROMANTIKK

One of Norway's most popular interior and thrift stores and Tilda's most faithful supporter of props.

www.landromantikk.no
Nedre Langgate 43, 3126 Tønsberg.
Phone: + 47 41 34 19 68

TORNEROSE

A flower shop that looks like a French backyard where you want everything you see. They also have really nice ladies serving behind the counter.

www.tornerose.as
Storgaten 41, 3126 Tønsberg.
Phone: + 47 33 33 17 33

MOWE

A pretty, whimsy, romantic and colourful store with a touch of the East. The staff are always friendly and helpful.

www.moweinterior.no
Storgaten 42, 3126 Tønsberg.
Phone: + 47 33 31 86 40

Patterns

Page references for the relevant patterns are listed in the project instruction pages.

Note: Add seam allowance to all parts in the pattern unless otherwise instructed.

SYMBOL EXPLANATION

ES: Extra seam allowance is very important here. Fold in by the inner dotted line, unless it is supposed to be stitched up with another piece, such as the legs for ballerinas or princesses. Always sew seam allowance that ends by an opening all the way out.

Dotted line: Marks the openings and indicates the border between two fabrics.

Folding edge: Means that the pattern should be reversed on the other side of the folding edge.

A–B: If the pattern is too big to fit a page and must be divided, A–B marks the points where one pattern page is supposed to be connected with another, so that A and B are facing each other.

COPYRIGHT

LETTERS "CHRISTMAS"

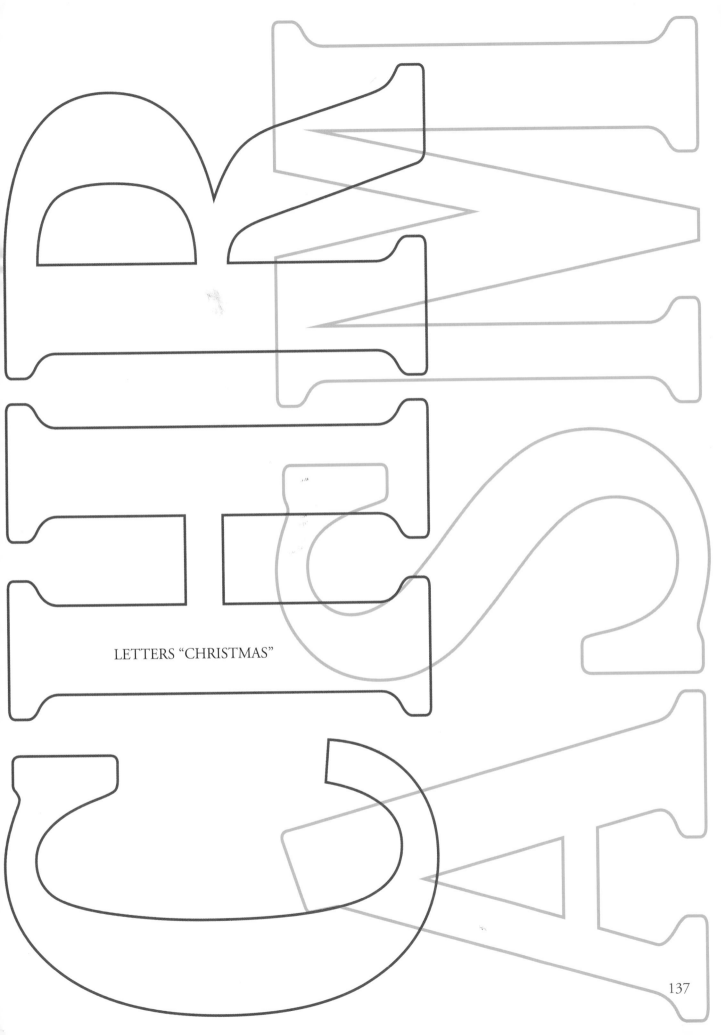

LETTERS "CHRISTMAS"

137

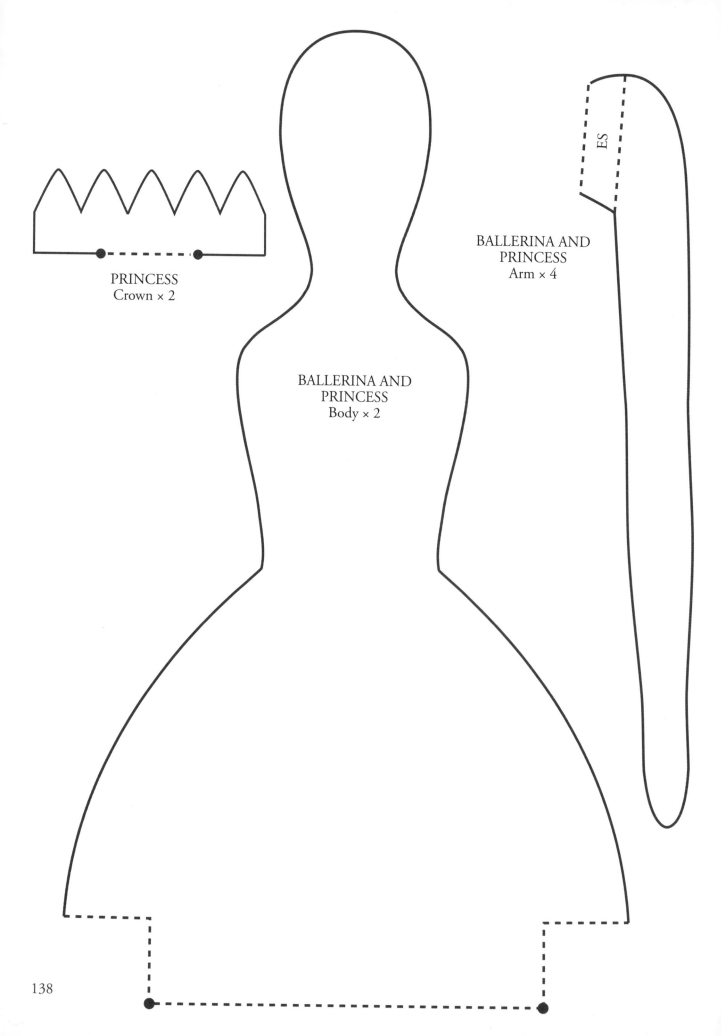

PRINCESS
Crown × 2

BALLERINA AND
PRINCESS
Arm × 4

BALLERINA AND
PRINCESS
Body × 2

ES

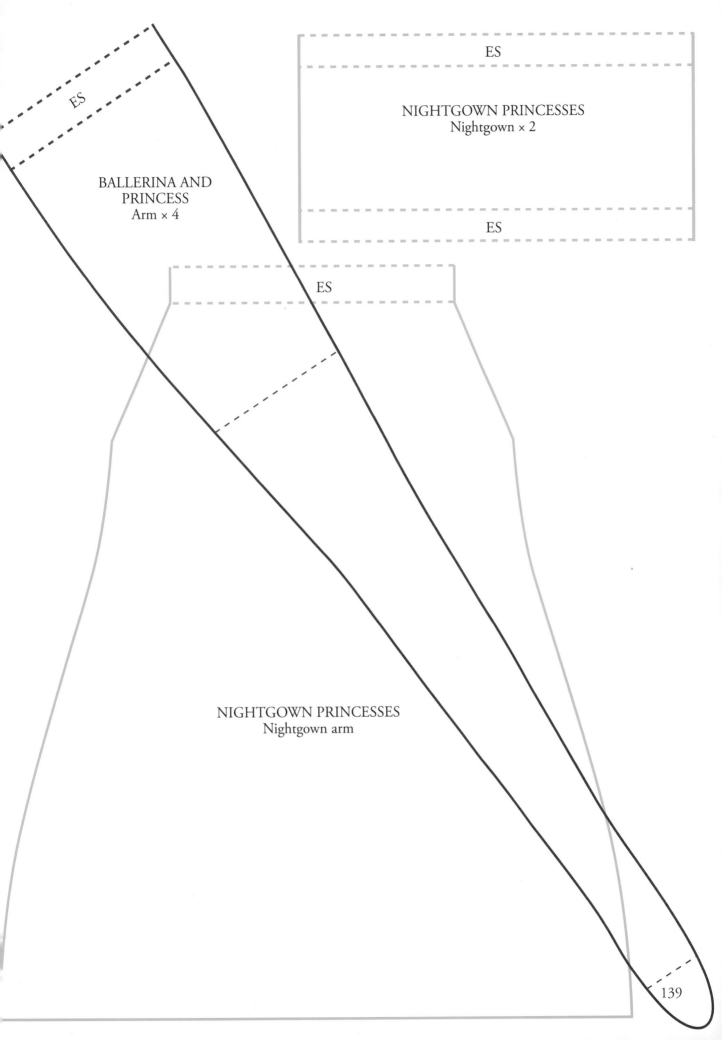

ES

BALLERINA AND
PRINCESS
Arm × 4

ES

NIGHTGOWN PRINCESSES
Nightgown × 2

ES

ES

NIGHTGOWN PRINCESSES
Nightgown arm

139

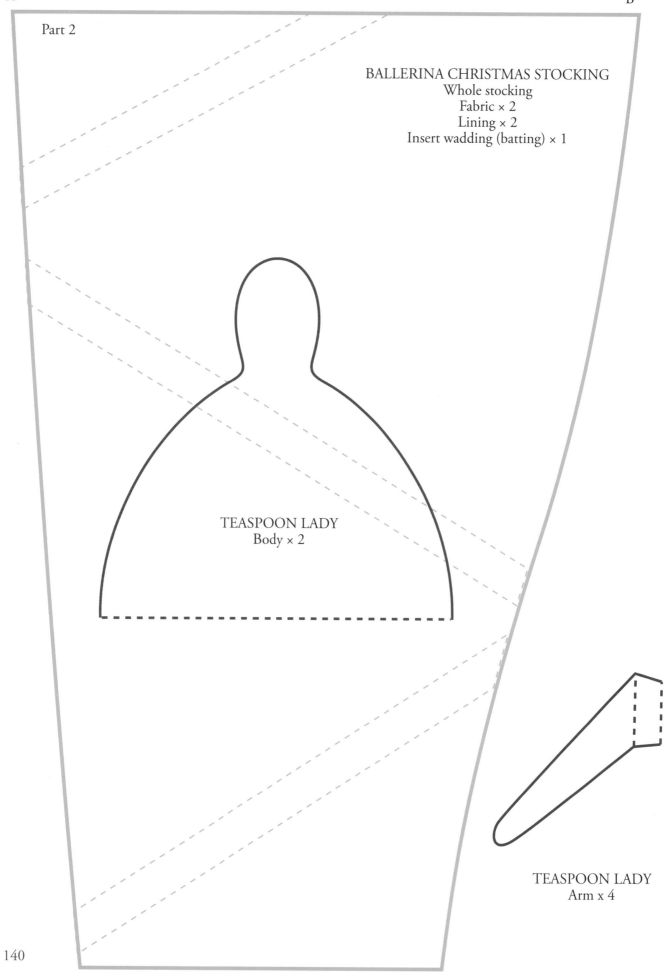

A

B

Part 2

BALLERINA CHRISTMAS STOCKING
Whole stocking
Fabric × 2
Lining × 2
Insert wadding (batting) × 1

TEASPOON LADY
Body × 2

TEASPOON LADY
Arm x 4

C

D

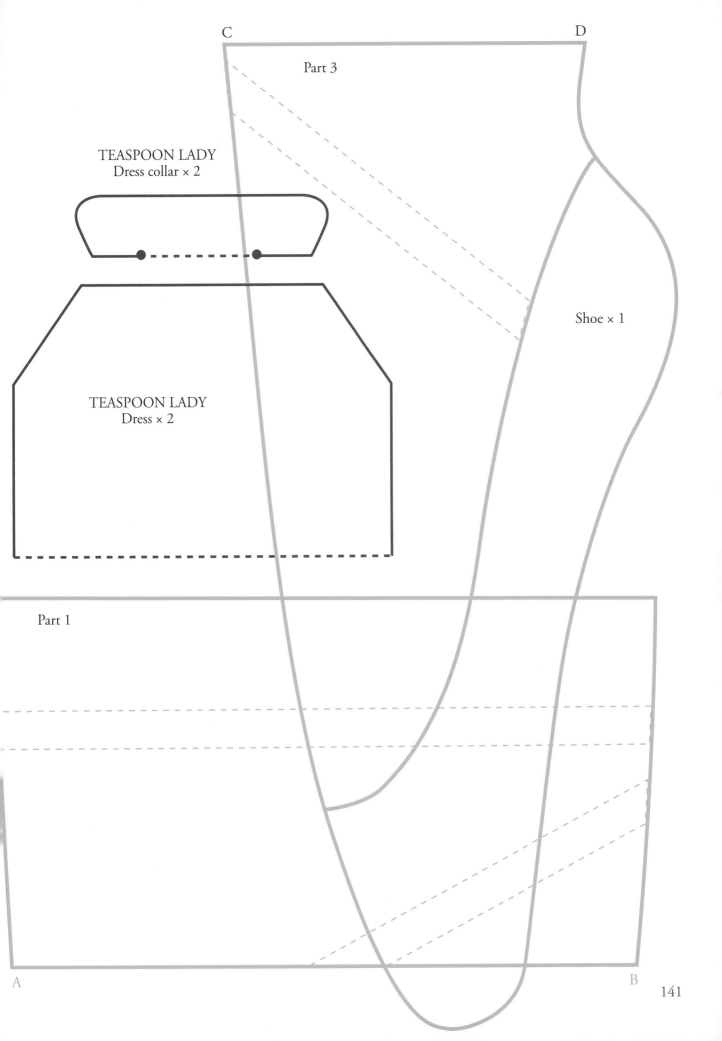

C

D

Part 3

TEASPOON LADY
Dress collar × 2

Shoe × 1

TEASPOON LADY
Dress × 2

Part 1

A

B

141

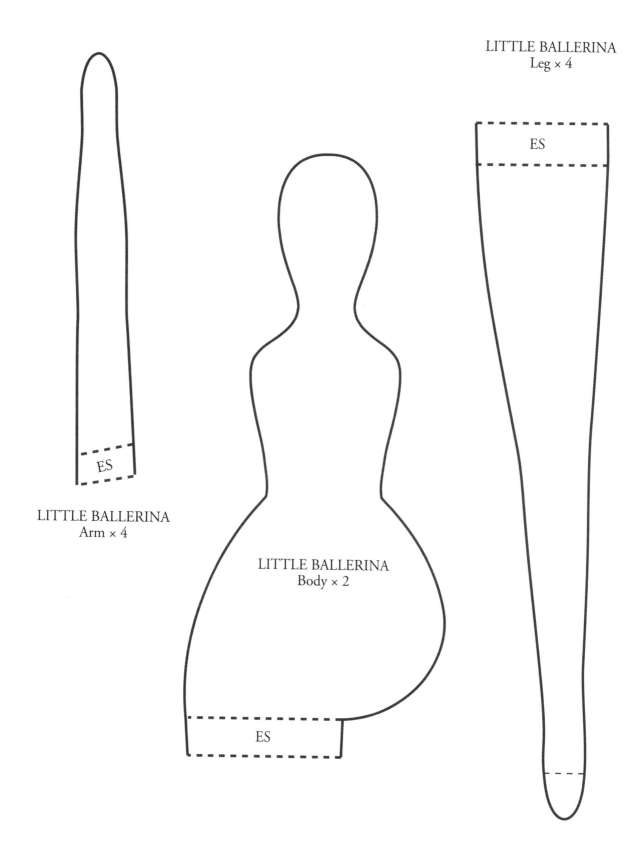

LITTLE BALLERINA
Leg × 4

ES

LITTLE BALLERINA
Arm × 4

ES

LITTLE BALLERINA
Body × 2

ES

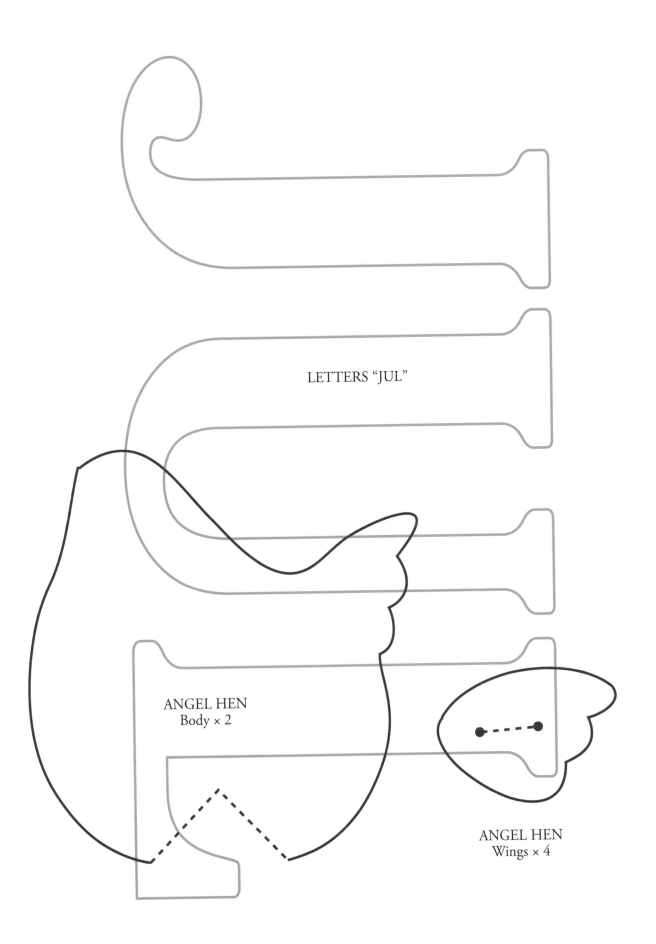

LETTERS "JUL"

ANGEL HEN
Body × 2

ANGEL HEN
Wings × 4

143

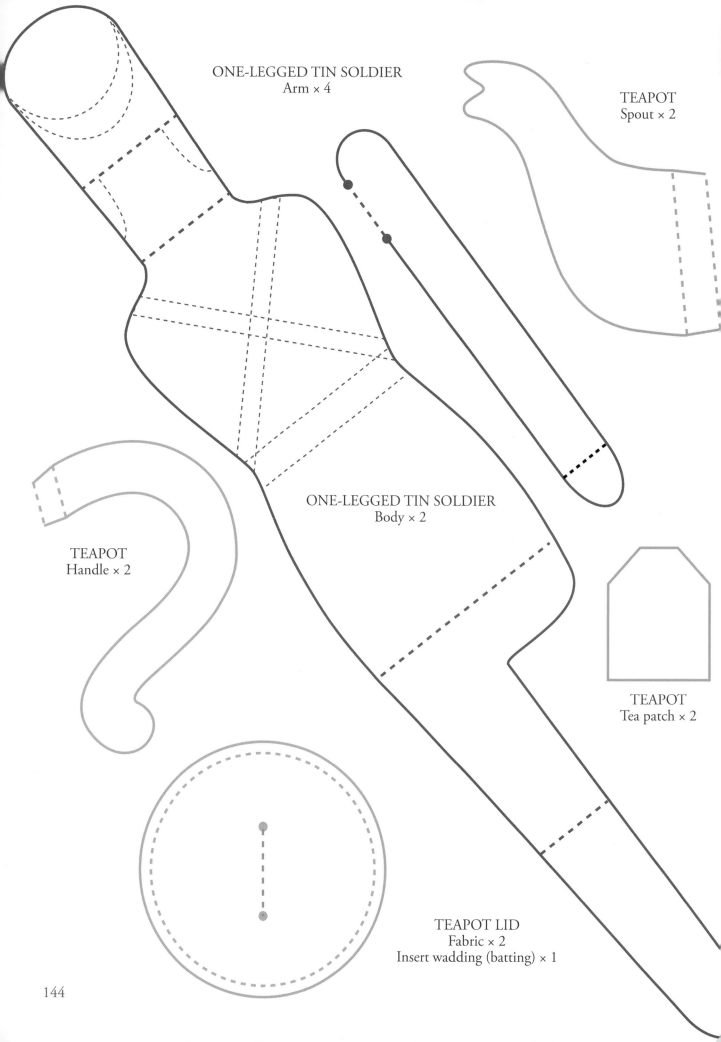

ONE-LEGGED TIN SOLDIER
Arm × 4

TEAPOT
Spout × 2

TEAPOT
Handle × 2

ONE-LEGGED TIN SOLDIER
Body × 2

TEAPOT
Tea patch × 2

TEAPOT LID
Fabric × 2
Insert wadding (batting) × 1

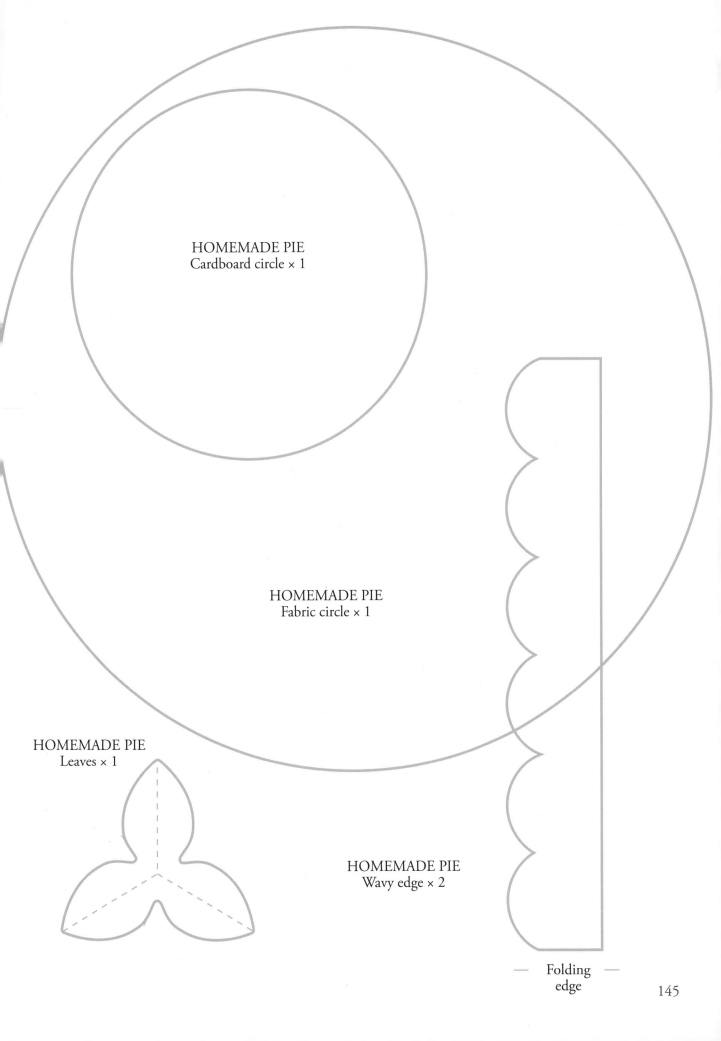

HOMEMADE PIE
Cardboard circle × 1

HOMEMADE PIE
Fabric circle × 1

HOMEMADE PIE
Leaves × 1

HOMEMADE PIE
Wavy edge × 2

Folding
edge

145

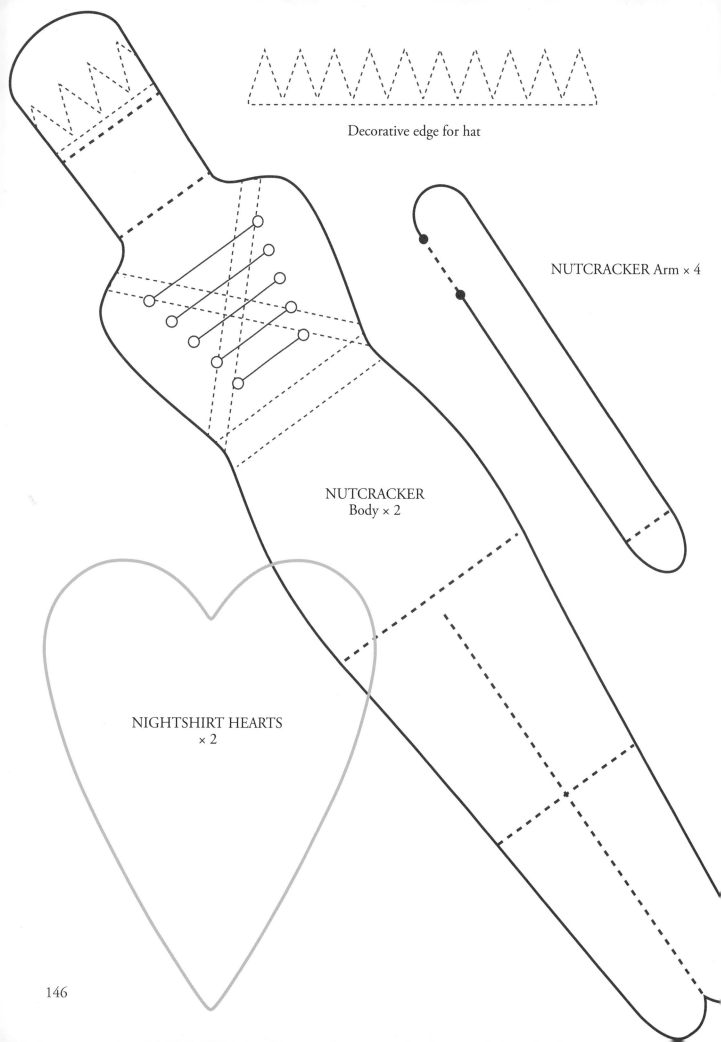

Decorative edge for hat

NUTCRACKER Arm × 4

NUTCRACKER
Body × 2

NIGHTSHIRT HEARTS
× 2

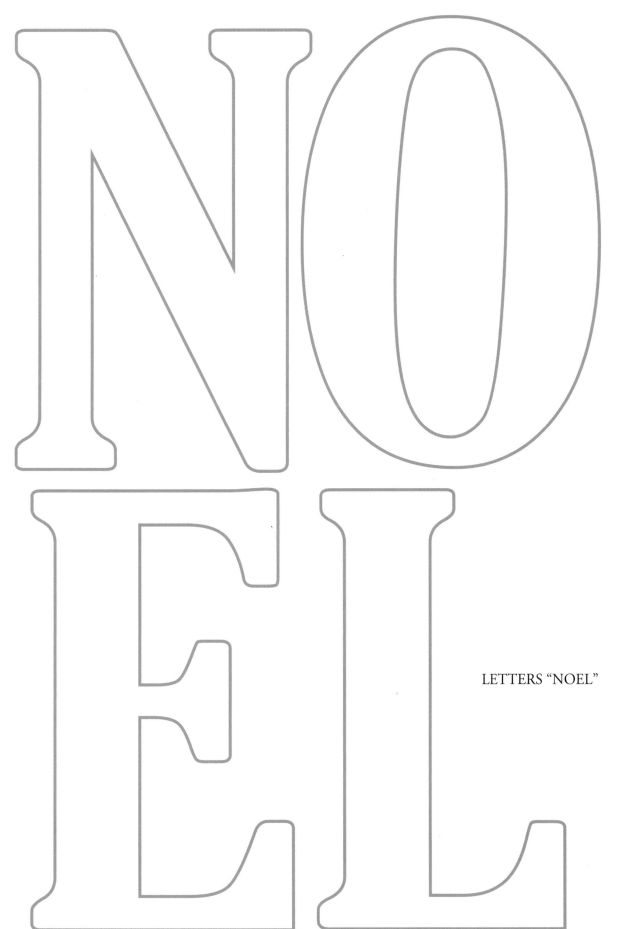

LETTERS "NOEL"

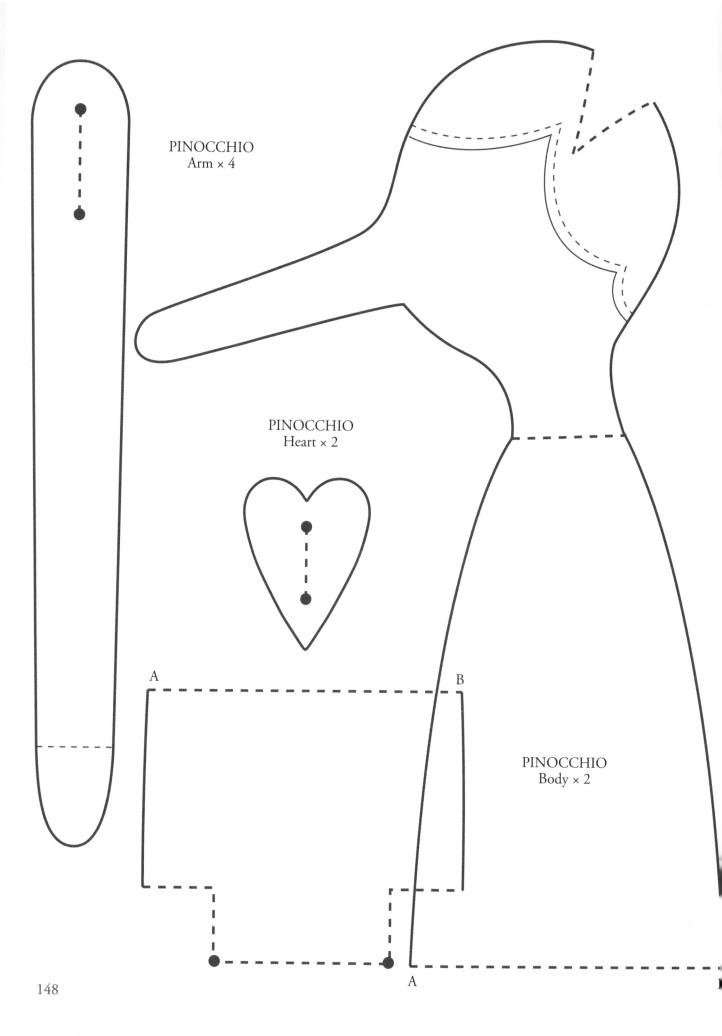

PINOCCHIO
Arm × 4

PINOCCHIO
Heart × 2

PINOCCHIO
Body × 2

A

B

A

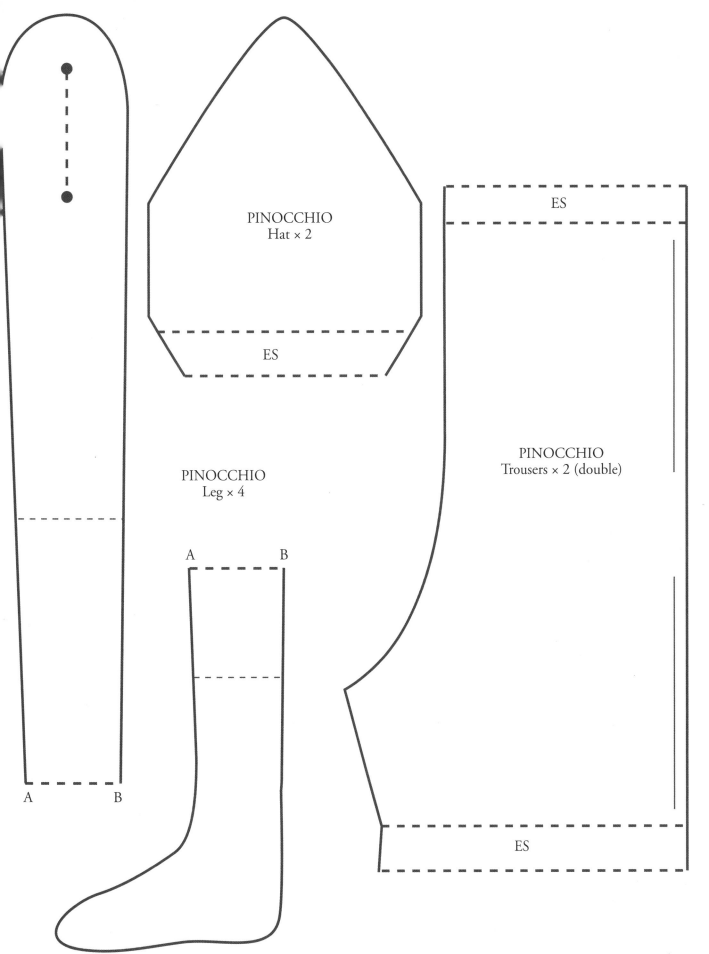

PINOCCHIO
Hat × 2

ES

ES

PINOCCHIO
Leg × 4

A   B

A

B

A   B

PINOCCHIO
Trousers × 2 (double)

ES

ES

149

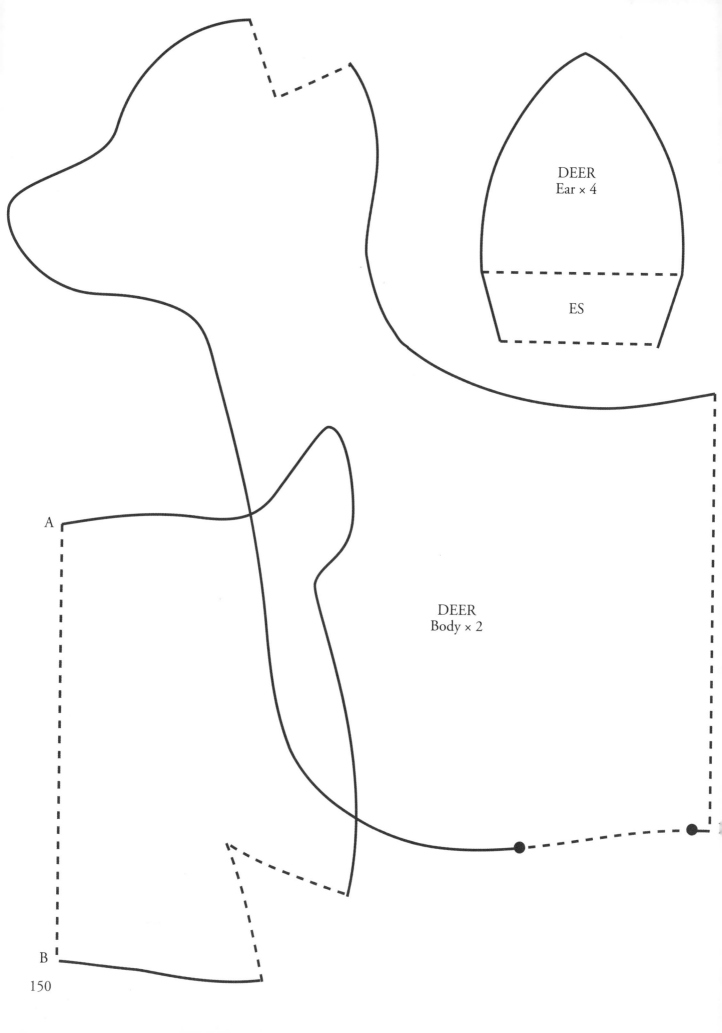

DEER
Ear × 4

ES

DEER
Body × 2

A

B

150

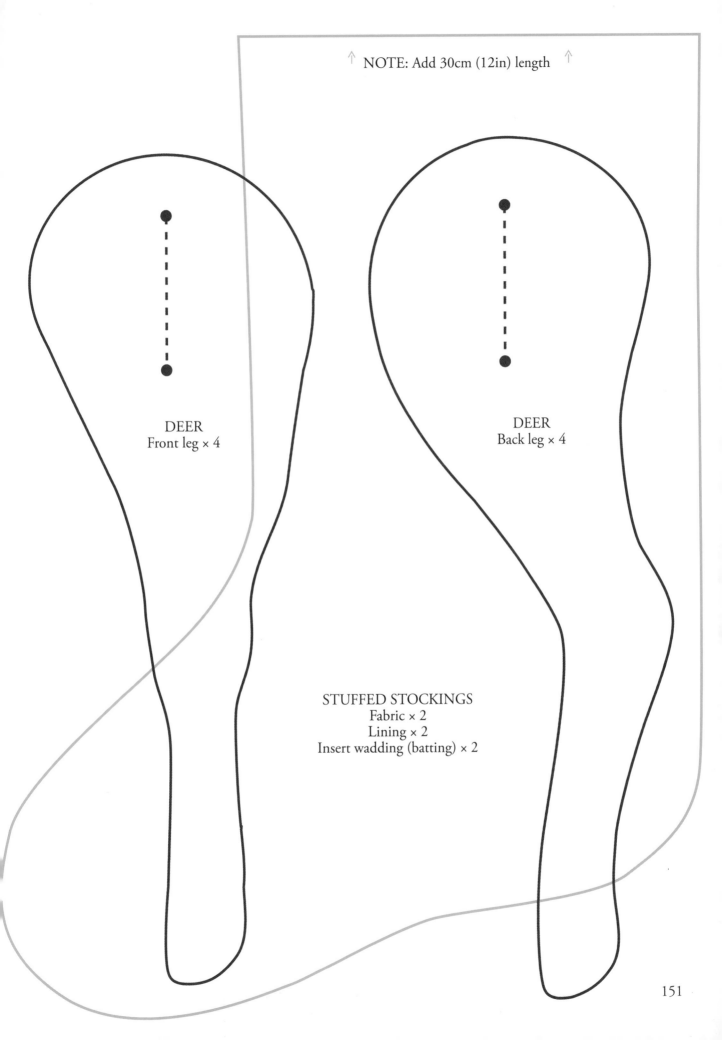

↑ NOTE: Add 30cm (12in) length ↑

DEER
Front leg × 4

DEER
Back leg × 4

STUFFED STOCKINGS
Fabric × 2
Lining × 2
Insert wadding (batting) × 2

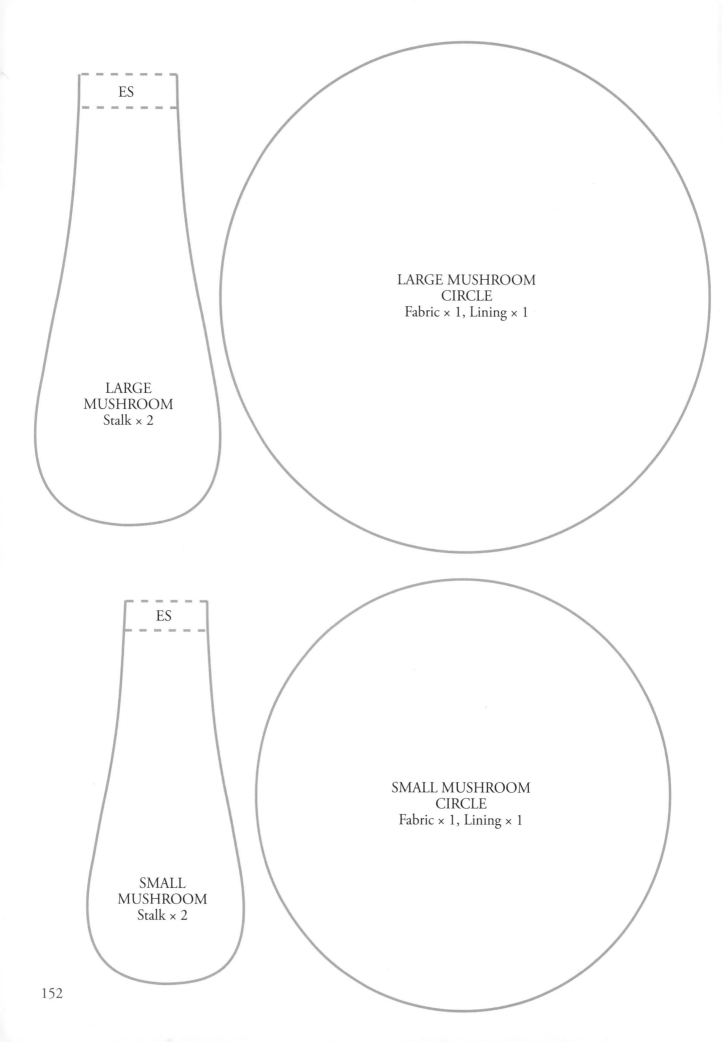

ES

LARGE
MUSHROOM
Stalk × 2

LARGE MUSHROOM
CIRCLE
Fabric × 1, Lining × 1

ES

SMALL
MUSHROOM
Stalk × 2

SMALL MUSHROOM
CIRCLE
Fabric × 1, Lining × 1

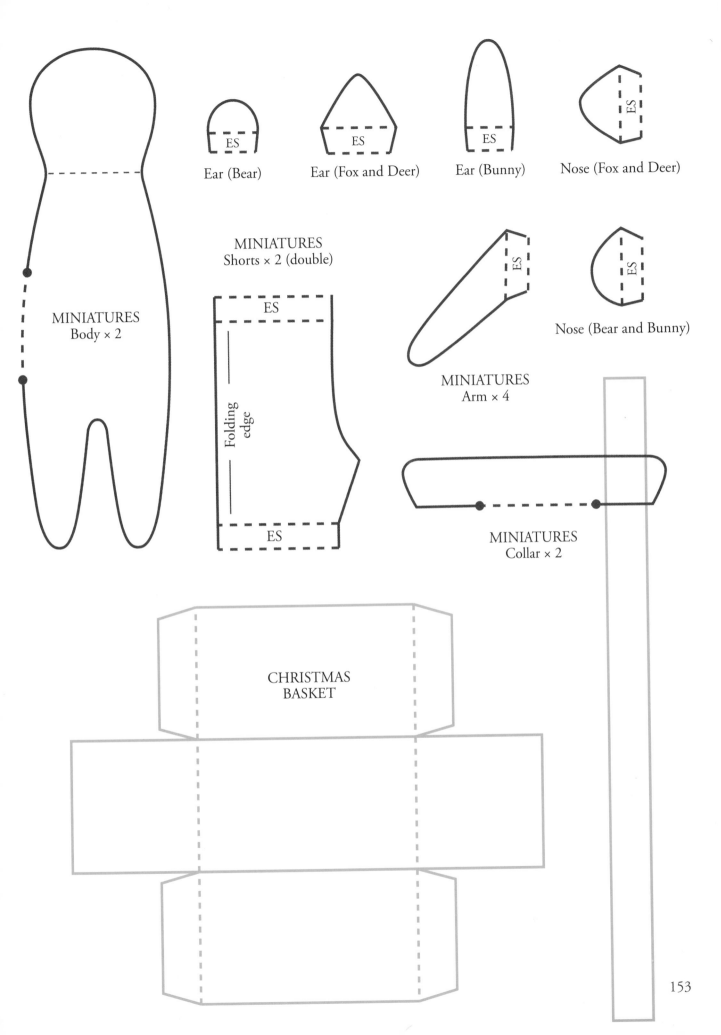

MINIATURES
Body × 2

Ear (Bear)

Ear (Fox and Deer)

Ear (Bunny)

Nose (Fox and Deer)

ES

ES

ES

ES

MINIATURES
Shorts × 2 (double)

ES

Folding edge

ES

ES

Nose (Bear and Bunny)

MINIATURES
Arm × 4

MINIATURES
Collar × 2

CHRISTMAS
BASKET

153

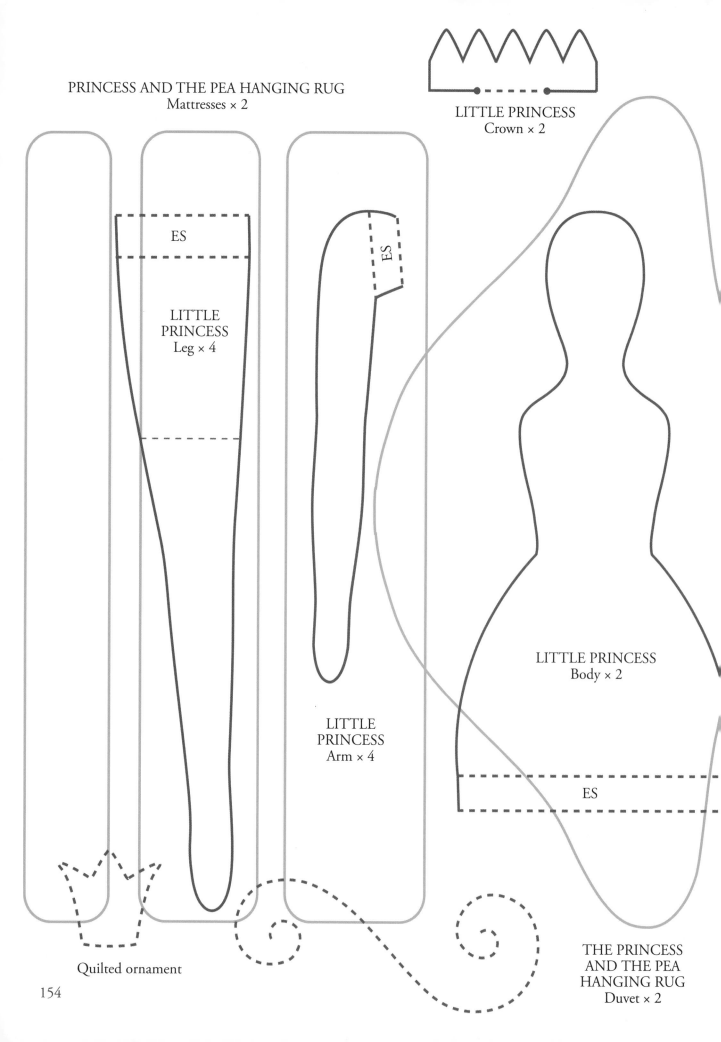

PRINCESS AND THE PEA HANGING RUG
Mattresses × 2

LITTLE PRINCESS
Crown × 2

ES

LITTLE
PRINCESS
Leg × 4

ES

LITTLE
PRINCESS
Arm × 4

LITTLE PRINCESS
Body × 2

ES

Quilted ornament

154

THE PRINCESS
AND THE PEA
HANGING RUG
Duvet × 2

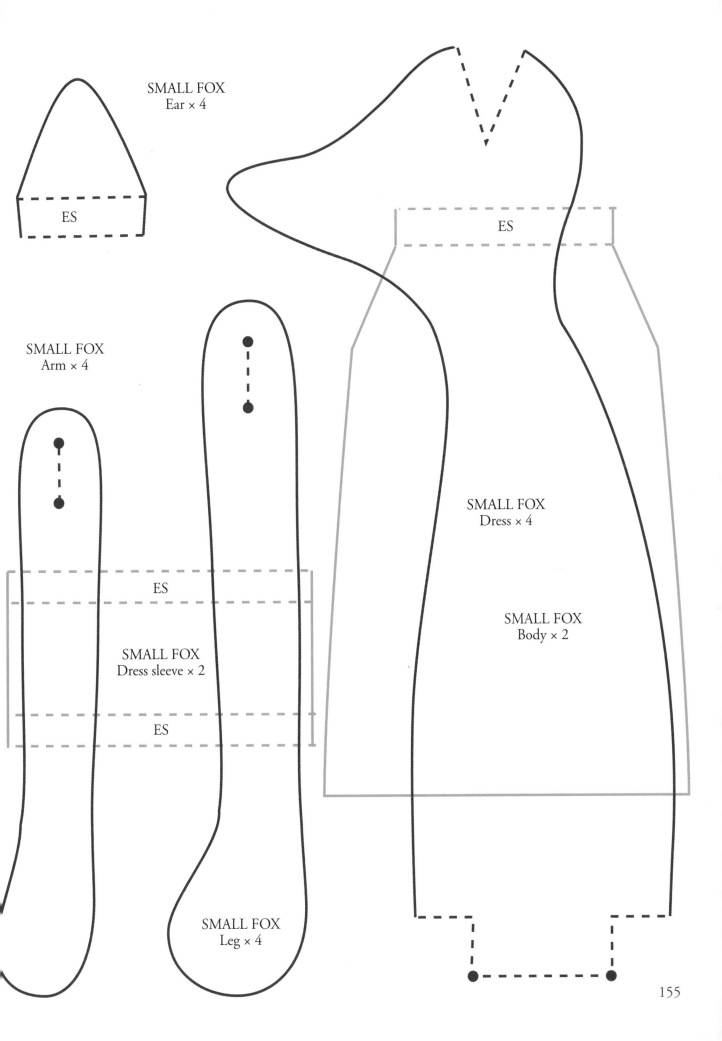

SMALL FOX
Ear × 4

ES

SMALL FOX
Arm × 4

ES

SMALL FOX
Dress sleeve × 2

ES

ES

SMALL FOX
Dress × 4

SMALL FOX
Body × 2

SMALL FOX
Leg × 4

155

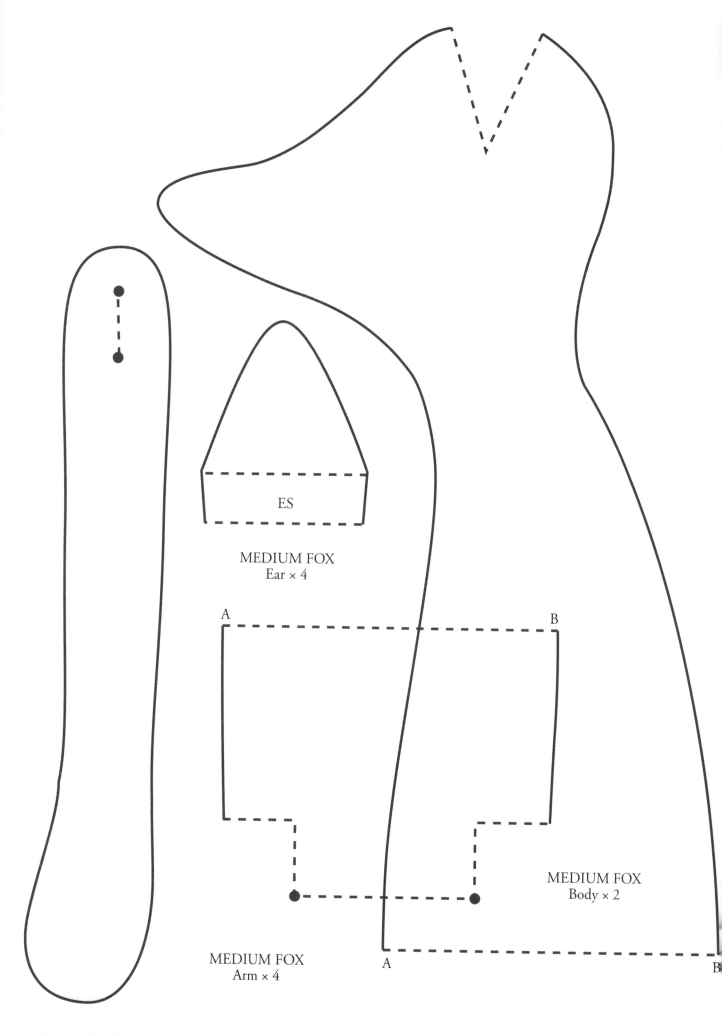

ES

MEDIUM FOX
Ear × 4

A

B

MEDIUM FOX
Body × 2

MEDIUM FOX
Arm × 4

A

B

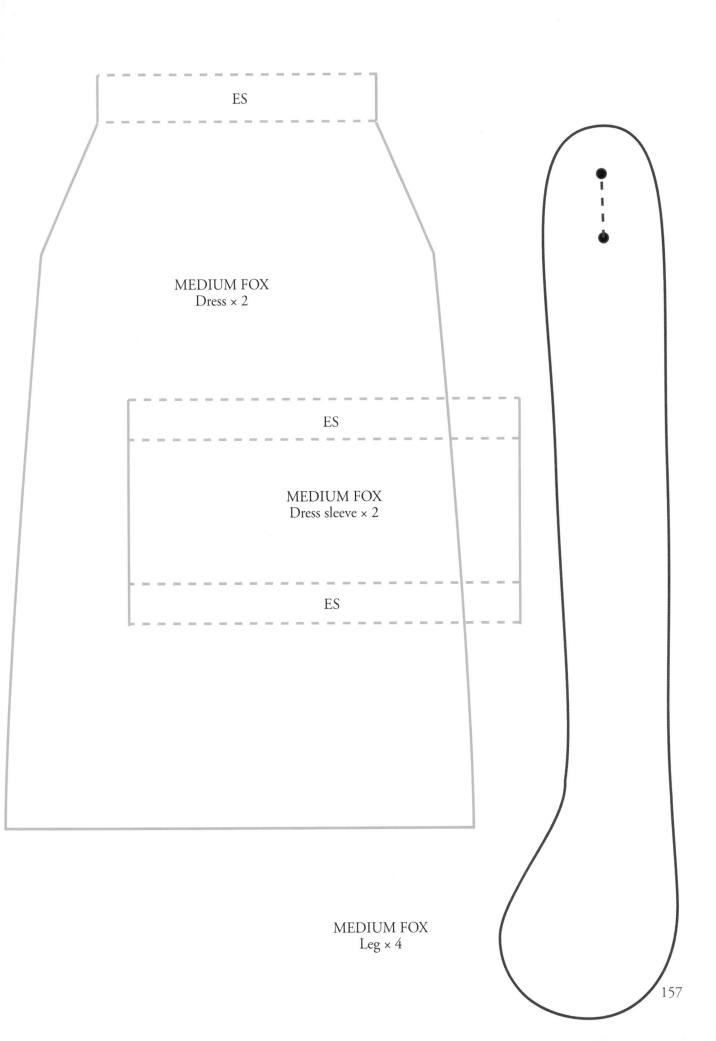

ES

MEDIUM FOX
Dress × 2

ES

MEDIUM FOX
Dress sleeve × 2

ES

MEDIUM FOX
Leg × 4

157

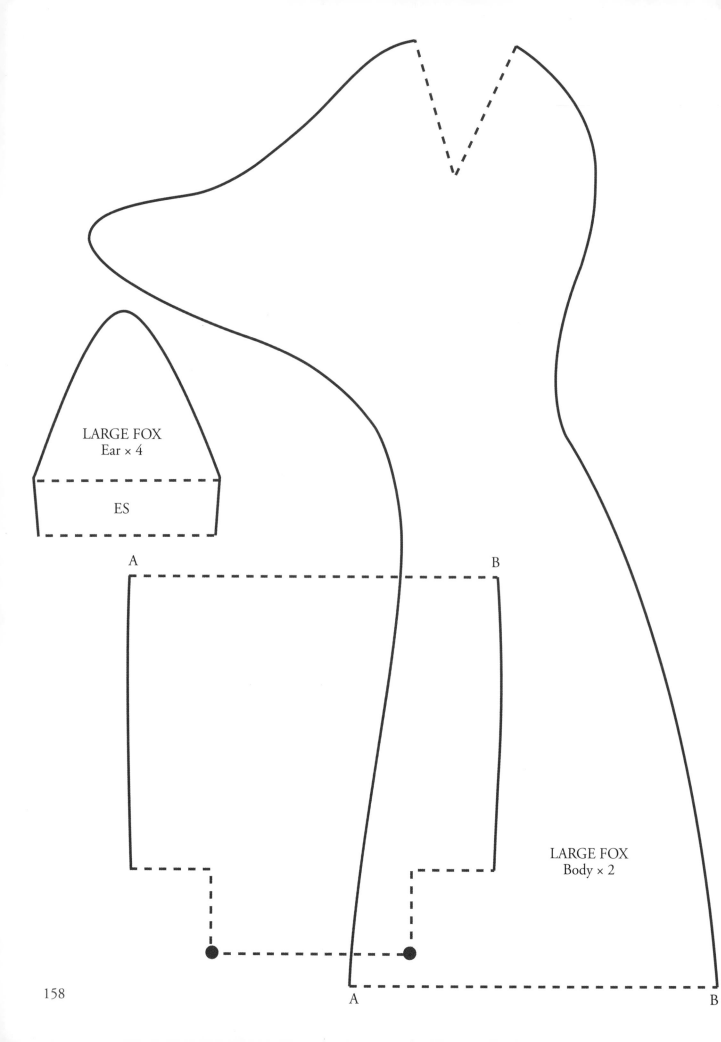

LARGE FOX
Ear × 4

ES

LARGE FOX
Body × 2

A

B

A

B

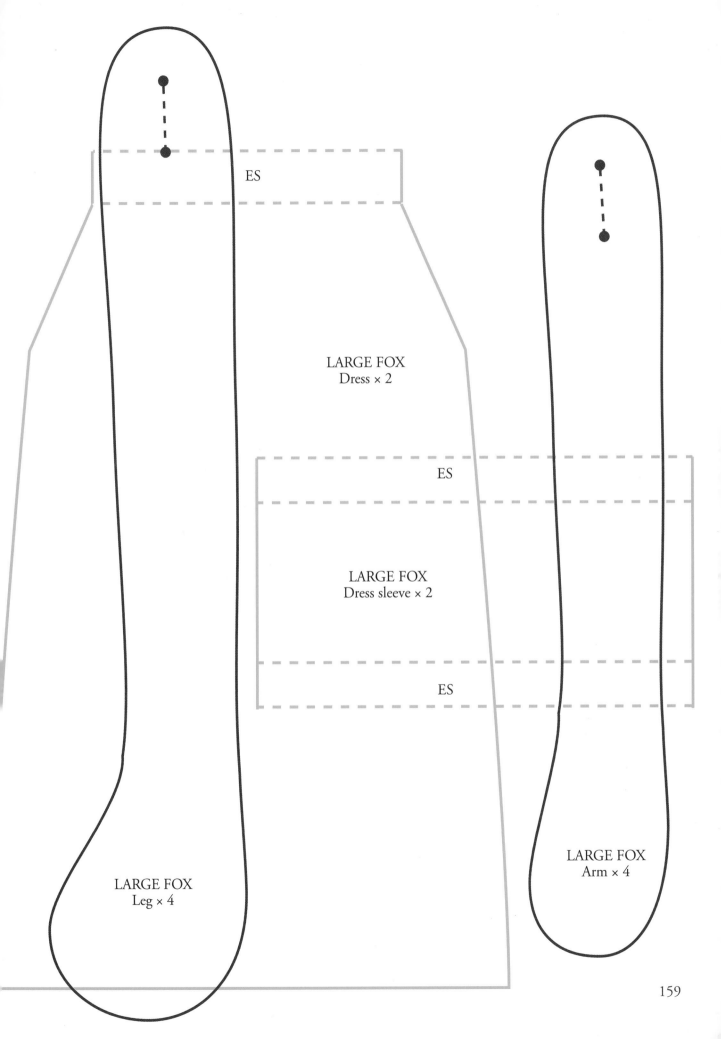

ES

LARGE FOX
Dress × 2

ES

LARGE FOX
Dress sleeve × 2

ES

LARGE FOX
Leg × 4

LARGE FOX
Arm × 4

Index

A DAVID & CHARLES BOOK
© Cappelen Damm AS 2012

Originally published in Norway as *Tildas Vintereventyr*
First published in the UK and USA in 2013 by F&W Media International, Ltd

David & Charles is an imprint of F&W Media International, Ltd
Brunel House, Forde Close, Newton Abbot, TQ12 4PU, UK

F&W Media International, Ltd is a subsidiary of F+W Media, Inc
10151 Carver Road, Suite #200, Blue Ash, OH 45242, USA

Tone Finnanger has asserted her right to be identified as author of this work in accordance with the Copyright, Designs and Patents Act, 1988.

The author and publisher have made every effort to ensure that all the instructions in the book are accurate and safe, and therefore cannot accept liability for any resulting injury, damage or loss to persons or property, however it may arise.

Names of manufacturers and product ranges are provided for the information of readers, with no intention to infringe copyright or trademarks.

A catalogue record for this book is available from the British Library.

ISBN-13: 978-1-4463-0331-3 paperback
ISBN-10: 1-4463-0331-4 paperback

Printed in China by RR Donnelley for F&W Media International, Ltd
Brunel House, Forde Close, Newton Abbot, TQ12 4PU, UK

10 9 8 7 6 5 4 3 2 1

Photographer: Sølvi Dos Santos
Stylist: Ingrid Skaansar
Illustrator: Tone Finnanger
Book design: Tone Finnanger

F+W Media publishes high quality books on a wide range of subjects. For more great book ideas visit:
www.stitchcraftcreate.co.uk